HOLY ROSARY

LEARNING TO PRAY USING THE ROSARY

EDWARD CARBEY

Copyright © 2019. EDWARD CARBEY All Rights Reserved.

No part of this publication may be reproduced, distributed, or transmitted in any form or by any means, including photocopying, recording, or other electronic or mechanical methods, or by any information storage and retrieval system without the prior written permission of the publisher, except in the case of very brief quotations embodied in critical reviews and certain other noncommercial uses permitted by copyright law.

All scripture quotations, unless otherwise noted, are taken from the King James Version of the Bible.

Scripture quotations marked NIV are taken from the HOLY BIBLE, NEW INTERNATIONAL VERSION, NIV. **Copyright © 1973, 1078, 1984 by International Bible Society. Used by**

Table of Contents

Chapter 1: Rosary And Christianity 1

Chapter 2: Rosary Basics 8

    Below Is A Simple Table Of Rosary Mysteries And Days The Rosary Is Prayed During Ordinary Time 11

    Easily Travel The Life Of Jesus Through Rosary Days And Liturgical Seasons 11

    History Of The Rosary: What Do Modern Popes Have To Say About The Rosary? 22

    Origin Of The Rosary: Where Does The Rosary Get Its Name? 24

    Power Of The Rosary Proves: That You Can Find Peace By Praying This Catholic Prayer 27

Chapter 3: Rosary Prayers 30

    How To Pray In Rosary 34

    Mondays And Saturdays 37

    A Practical Guide On How To Pray The Rosary 39

Chapter 4: Rosary Mysteries 43

    The Joyful Mysteries 45

    The Luminous Mysteries 58

    The Sorrowful Mysteries 68

    The Scourging At The Pillar 71

    The Crowning With Thorns 73

    The Carrying Of The Cross 75

    The Crucifixion 77

    The Glorious Mysteries 79

    The Resurrection Of Jesus Christ 79

The Ascension Of Jesus To Heaven............................81

The Descent Of The Holy Ghost (Pentecost).............84

The Assumption Of The Blessed Virgin Mary Into Heaven..87

The Coronation Of The Blessed Virgin Mary, Queen Of Heaven And Earth..89

Chapter 5: Power And Personal Testimonies Of The Rosary Personal Testimonies Of The Rosary.................92

The Power Of The Rosary In Converting Protestants 92

Conclusion..125

CHAPTER 1
ROSARY AND CHRISTIANITY

In Christianity, Catholics use the Rosary in order to demonstrate their dedication to Jesus' mother, Mary. The rosary itself can be through both a tangible set of beads and through a practice of a devotion ritual. The beads themselves are used as a physical reminder of counting time and keep track of the prayers said during the ritual. The rosary as a material object is usually made up of five sections of ten beads, each section separated by a larger bead. It is constructed like a necklace. The main part has three small beads along with two larger beads and an enclosed pendant.

Rosaries can be found in all forms and types, in various shades and can be made with many types of material. The term rosary, when described as a ritual, contains a repeating of three prayers together along with a recitation of beliefs. This practice can be completed by any person, in any context, whether in a group or alone. The rosary might very well be an non-discriminatory practice where people from all faiths can participate. It can even be said in any location, but ideally in a Catholic worship space, such as the church.

The history of the Rosary is not altogether clear. Our Lady Mary gave the Rosary to St. Dominic (1170 – 1221), at the beginning of the 13th century to help combat the Albigensian heresy in France. (The heresy which is the purposeful denial of the divinity of Christ.) Custom also holds that she promised Dominic his Order would blossom if he spread dedication to the Rosary. Whether or not this is true, it is unlikely that the Rosary he had exactly resembles the one we use today. Many scholars sustain that the history of the Rosary most likely comes from a long and gradual process starting before St. Dominic's life and continuing to the 15th century. Eventually, they believe, 50 Hail Marys were recited and thus this form of prayer became known as the 'rosarium,' a rose garden.

The devotion that we use today is for the most part made up of a prayer directly from the Bible, with the beginning portion of the Hail Mary recounting the words of the Archangel Gabriel, who called Mary 'full of grace'; the second part of the salutation comes from the mouth of her cousin Elizabeth, who said: 'Blessed art thou among women, and blessed is the fruit of thy womb!'

Looking beyond the language to the mystery itself, the Rosary has been described as the life, ministry and calling of Jesus, directly provided for us by the Virgin Mary herself with meditative and prayerful purposes, allowing us to learn who Jesus is.

Altogether it is a precious thread that connects us to the Son of God.

The traditional 15 mysteries were solidified by Pope St. Pius V in the 16th century. He introduced the Rosary into the Roman Catholic liturgical calendar, deeming the 7th of October as the Feast day of 'Our Lady of the Rosary.' (He would have been honored to learn that she since then described this as her preferred title.)

In his papal encyclical at the time, he wrote, 'This devotion in its origin and wisdom is more divine than human.'

Much advice and encouragement has been given regarding the use of this particular from of devotion. It has been supported by popes, and even a quite large number of saints. Somewhat recently, Pope John Paul II described the Rosary as his favorite prayer, noting that it can be prayed by both laymen and theologians; saying that 'through the Rosary the faithful receive abundant grace, as though from the hands of the Redeemer.'

The Rosary is not mandatory, and we are not forced to say it, but to evade is a complete loss and miss of an enriching prayer, that which is particularly encouraged and practiced by Our Lady Mary herself. It may be slightly difficult to hold attention to the prayers while meditating on the happenings of the mysteries, but we should not allow the words to take over and conquer while contemplating the events of the Gospel, as well as the other way around. It is not something to be worried about. For example, when we focus on the suffering of the Crucifixion, the words might become hazy as we are meditating on the terrible pain and suffering of Our Lord. This is how it is supposed to be.

The Rosary can be said alone or with others. For those wishing to take advantage of outside encouragement there is The Living Rosary Association, formed originally in 1826 by Pauline Jaricot to save the church in France. It was formally approved by Pope Gregory XVI in 1832. Although it lost momentum it was revived on the 8th of December, 1986, by the husband and wife team of Richard and Patricia Melvin in America. Today, more than 12 million faithful servants are joined worldwide through The Living Rosary, united with Mary in prayer to hasten the triumph of her Immaculate Heart and to bring about the reign of Christ the King.

Within Catholicism, the rosary is known as to be a symbolic item and also an informal practice. The first overall look of the physical group of beads is early on within the religion and can be seen in a variety of images depicting early on practitioners. The ritual itself can be regarded as secondary method of devotion (primary becoming sacraments and liturgy) that could be completed at one's private will. Although takes action of praying the rosary isn't formal in the feeling that it is not really a requirement, it acts as a meditative approach to prayer for those trying to find a deeper spiritual faith.

The praying of the rosary traces its origins to the Book of Psalms contained within the Bible. Catholics consider psalms as worship tracks to God. Through the beginning of Catholicism, most lay people desired to partake in the praying of the Psalms but could not commit all 150 to memory, thus there arrived a substitute. In the early sixteenth century, we have evidence of a publication titled the Chiropsalterium, which taught practitioners to use their physical hands as a mnemonic device while praying, also including 150 repetitions of the Our fathers as substitutions for the psalms. The Our Daddy is considered to be the epitome of all prayers, because it was created for our needs by our Lord himself, as John S. Johnson stated himself. He then continues to say that, in the Gospel of Matthew in the Holy Bible, Jesus taught that this must be the method of how one prays to God. With a few alterations, Catholics today use these texts and consider it the Lord's Prayer.

As Catholicism grew immensely, so did a need for meditations in parallel to Jesus' life, and thus it was out of convenience that each of the three sets of 50 were quite soon decreased to groups of 10, each mystery holding five important events connected with a biblical motif. It was St. Dominic, who through the fifteenth century, who was attributed to the discovery of what's now known as the Rosary.

According to legend, Mary is thought to have revealed herself to him, advising him to spread the words contained within the Psalter; which then formalized to the three mysteries, five years in each. Only recently, in 2002, was the 4th mystery added by the Pope completing what we now know as the Catholic Rosary.

The purpose of the Rosary is to solidify in memory the most importnat events in the history of our salvation, these of which are divided into the five Joyful Mysteries (to be said on Monday and Saturday), the five Luminous Mysteries (to be said on Thursday), the five Sorrowful Mysteries (said on Tuesday and Friday), and the five Glorious Mysteries (said on Wednesday and Sunday). There are a couple of exceptions. During Christmas, the Joyful Mysteries are said instead on Sundays, and the Sorrowful Mysteries are said during the Sundays of Lent.

Many wonder why, of all of the events of Jesus' life, does the Rosary only confront these specific twenty. The mysteries of the rosary are based on life events that Our Lord and His Mother experienced, specifically those which are celebrated in the Liturgy. The twenty mysteries of the Rosary thus reflect the main feasts that celebrate our Lord and his Mother in the liturgical year. Thus, when one recites the twenty mysteries of the Rosary in one day, they are prayerfully producing the whole annual liturgical cycle of the Church. This is why some Popes have called the Rosary a compilation of the gospel itself.

The first part of the rosary is made up of the Creed, Our father, and three Hail Marys.

Hail Marys comes from the two greetings to Mary in the gospel of Luke: "Hail, the Lord if with thee," and "Blessed art thou amongst women and blessed is the fruit of thy womb." (Course and change translation)

The rosary prayer beads came much later than the rosary itsel. The purpose of the rosary beads are to keep count of how many Hail Marys are being said as one contemplates the mysteries; fingers moving along beads as prayers are lifted. This counting guide allows one's mind to fully meditate on the mysteries rather than being distracted by numbers.

The purpose of this book is to go through the holy prayers of the Rosary: that including, The Luminous Mysteries, The Sorrowful Mysteries, and the Glorious Mysteries. After getting to know the prayers of each Mystery, you will then find a practical guide on how to pray the Rosary.

Chapter 2:
Rosary Basics

What is the Rosary?

The term "The Rosary" refers to both a prayer and a physical object. The physical object is a set of Rosary beads. The prayer involves using the Rosary beads to keep track of where you are. (It's a long prayer.)

Therefore, I'll use the term "Rosary beads" to refer to the physical object, and "the Rosary" to refer to the prayer.

The Rosary is a simple prayer. It takes just a couple of minutes to learn how to pray the Rosary.

Its basic structure is:

- An introduction (a few brief prayers)
- A series of five decades, each contemplating a mystery of the Christian faith
- A conclusion (another few brief prayers)

What's a "decade"?

The main loop of a set of Rosary beads is divided into five decades. Each decade has a single bead, a space, and then ten beads.

You follow the beads with your fingers as you say each prayer.

When you starts a decade, you name the mystery for it. (Don't worry — there's a list of them you'll follow!) Then you say an Our father on the single bead, followed by ten Hail Marys, one for each of the ten beads. Then you end the decade with a Glory Be.

Well, it's all about the mystery for that decade. These are the central mysteries of the Christian faith: the Nativity, the Crucifixion, the Resurrection, etc.

When you learn how to pray the Rosary, you learn about prayer itself.

As you say the prayers, you think about the current decade's mystery. The Rosary is actually a combination of all three main forms of Christian prayer: vocal, meditation, and contemplation.

- It's vocal prayer because you're constantly saying the words of some prayers.
- It's meditative prayer because you're using Christian meditation to pray, using both the mystery and the words of the vocal prayers as source material.
- It's contemplative prayer because sometimes you also just sit in a kind of inner silence with Mary, just watching Christ and being in love, contemplating his love for us in the mystery at hand.

The beauty of the Rosary is that it easily lets you move back and forth among these three types of prayer. When the vocal prayer becomes routine, you let your mind wander to the mystery. When your attention wanders in meditation, you can fix its focus on the words of the prayers. All the while, your fingers move in a slow rhythm over the beads, keeping track of where you are, leading you to the next vocal prayer.

It is a deeply peaceful prayer.

Learning how to pray the Rosary will bring a beautiful period of peace into your daily life. \

Rosary Days For Praying

*"All things have their season...A time to weep, and a time to laugh.
A time to mourn, and a time to dance...A time to keep silence,
and a time to speak...A time of love, and a time of hatred.
A time of war, and a time of peace."-Ecclesiastes 3:1,4,7-8*

The Catholic Church has set aside Rosary days to help aid you in praying the Rosary. There are also different times of the year during church seasons such as Lent and Advent that have a slightly different order to pray the Rosary. This page will help you determine which mysteries of the rosary for which days they are prayed upon.

The cycle of the Rosary follows the rhythm of the liturgical year observed by the Catholic Church.

Below is a simple table of Rosary mysteries and days the Rosary is prayed during ordinary time:

- Sunday - Glorious Mysteries of the Rosary
- Monday - Joyful Mysteries of the Rosary
- Tuesday - Sorrowful Mysteries of the Rosary
- Wednesday - Glorious Mysteries of the Rosary
- Thursday - Luminous Mysteries of the Rosary
- Friday - Sorrowful Mysteries of the Rosary
- Saturday - Joyful Mysteries of the Rosary

Easily Travel The Life Of Jesus Through Rosary Days And Liturgical Seasons

The Catholic Rosary prayers beautifully accompany the various seasons within the Church year.

These special Catholic prayers are adjusted during the seasons of Christmas and Lent.

In the Christmas season, the Joyful Mysteries are prayed on Sundays. Likewise, during the season of Lent, the Sorrowful Mysteries are prayed on Sundays. Thereby giving emphasis to the events in the life of Jesus that are being celebrated during those two seasons of the year.

His incarnation and birth during Christmas and His passion and death during Lent.

Rosary Promises

The following rewards of the Rosary promises are very valuable, since we must cooperate with God's grace in order to earn eternal life. They enable us to accept God's grace and follow His commands more readily.

Mary made *15 promises* to those who say the Rosary daily. You will find them below plus the meaning of each one.

She told these promises to St. Dominic:

- To all those who shall pray my Rosary devoutly, I promise my special protection and great graces. What a consoling thought, having the Queen of Heaven and earth's special protection.
- Those who shall persevere in the recitation of my Rosary will receive some special grace. As you can see, you must persevere and say the Rosary daily to receive these promises.
- The Rosary will be a very powerful armor against hell; it will destroy vice, deliver from sin and dispel heresy. Just imagine the serenity and peace that comes from knowing for certain you are going to heaven. Sin hurts your soul and in the long run makes, you unhappy.

- Being a slave to your vices is unbearable. Mary will keep you safe from your own bad habits.
- How reassuring to know you will be free from falling for false teachings especially during these times when as St. Paul says in his second letter to Timothy, *"For there shall be a time, when they will not endure sound doctrine; but, according to their own desires, they will heap to themselves teachers, having itching ears"-2 Timothy 4:3*
- The Rosary will make virtue and good works flourish, and will obtain for souls the most abundant divine mercies. It will draw the hearts of men from the love of the world and its vanities, and will lift them to the desire of eternal things. Oh, that souls would sanctify themselves by this means.
- Divine mercies describe the mercy of Jesus. When you die He will bestow His boundless mercy upon you.
- Knowing that you will be treated with the utmost love and forgiveness can bring much comfort when reviewing your mistakes and shortcomings.
- Mary greatly desires that we become more holy by praying the Rosary everyday. This promise complements what St. Paul says in Romans 12:3. *"And*

be not conformed to this world; but be reformed in the newness of your mind, that you may prove what is the good, and the acceptable, and the perfect will of God."-Romans 12:3

- Those who trust themselves to me through the Rosary will not perish.
- Whoever recites my Rosary devoutly reflecting on the mysteries, shall never be overwhelmed by misfortune. He will not experience the anger of God nor will he perish by an unprovided death. The sinner will be converted; the just will persevere in grace and merit eternal life.
- You may experience misfortune, but you can rest assured that you will never be overwhelmed by it. By "un-provided death" the promise means that your soul will be prepared for the final judgement before you die.
- Those truly devoted to my Rosary shall not die without the sacraments of the Church. This is truly a wonderful promise. Last Rites is one of the seven sacraments.
- When a person is sick or injured, and in danger, of dying they receive this sacrament. It involves the certain prayers and anointing with holy oil by a priest. Sometimes, the recipient's health is regained. But even if they do not get well

- they will experience an increase of grace and they will be strengthened against temptation.
- The most important benefit of receiving this sacrament is that it prepares you to enter into heaven by forgiving your sins and cleaning your soul which has been stained due to the effects of sin. *"Is any one among you sick? Let him bring in the presbyters of the Church, and let them pray over him, anointing him with oil in the name of the Lord. And the prayer of faith will save the sick man, and the Lord will raise him up, and if he be in sins, they shall be forgiven him." -James 5:14-15*
- By this promise, you can be confident, and rest assured that you will receive this very important and beneficial sacrament before you die.
- Those who are faithful to recite my Rosary shall have during their life and at their death the light of God and the plenitude of His graces and will share in the merits of the blessed.
- Nothing can be more reassuring than this promise that give the hope of spending a life and particularly at the moment of death, being showered with God's grace and receiving the prayers of the saints already in heaven.

- I will deliver promptly from purgatory souls devoted to my Rosary.
- Purgatory is a place of cleansing. It is God's mudroom. Here you will be cleansed of all the effects that sin has caused in your soul. The most horrible thing about purgatory is the fact that you know God, but you cannot be with Him. This longing is agonizing. Yet it is very joyful because you know that you will eventually go to heaven, it's just a matter of time.
- Here Mary promises that your time there will be brief.
- True children of my Rosary will enjoy great glory in heaven.
- What you shall ask through my Rosary you shall obtain. Stressed? Worried? Anxious? Pray the Rosary every day. If you persevere in this, ALL you ask, you will receive.
- To those who propagate my Rosary I promise aid in all their necessities. You will be assisted in all your needs if you encourage others to pray the Rosary.
- Help share this wonderful tool that has brought so much peace and serenity into your life.
- Teach it to your family. Tell your friends about this book. If your life has been

impacted please share this with those you love.
- I have obtained from my Son that all the members of the Rosary Confraternity shall have as their intercessors, in life and in death, the entire celestial court.
- Because Mary is our Advocate, she assists us during our life and at our death.
- The Celestial Court is better known as the Communion of Saints. The Saints already in heaven pray for us on earth. All the Saints will ask God to supply for your needs if you become a member of the Rosary Confraternity.
- The Rosary Confraternity [new window will open] is a world-wide group whose members pray the fifteen decade Rosary at least once a week. It is entrusted to the Dominican order, the order of priests founded by St. Dominic.
- Since the Holy Father has recently added the five luminous mysteries, we encourage members of the Confraternity to include that extra weekly Rosary.
- However, we have as yet received no official statement regarding this matter. Those who recite only the fifteen traditional mysteries will continue to share in the benefits of the Confraternity until some official source declares the contrary. *"Whenever a person fulfills his*

obligation of reciting the Rosary according to the rule of the Confraternity, he includes in his intentions all its members, and they, in turn, render him the same service many times over." -Pope Leo XIII

- Each member includes deceased fellow members as well; and thus he knows that in turn, he will be included in the prayers of hundreds of thousands both now and hereafter.
- This led the Cure of Ars to say: *"If anyone has the happiness of being in the Confraternity of the Rosary, he has in all corners of the world brothers and sisters who pray for him."* - Cure of Ars
- Those who recite my Rosary faithfully are my beloved children, the brothers, and sisters of Jesus Christ.
- Devotion to my Rosary is a special sign of predestination. Predestination in this context means that, by the sign which is present to a person from the action of devoutly praying the Rosary, God has pre-ordained your salvation.
- Absolute certainty of salvation can only be truly known if God reveals it to a person because although we are given sufficient Grace during life, our salvation depends upon our response to said, Grace.

- Said another way, if God has guaranteed a person's salvation but has not revealed it to Him, God would want that person to pray the Rosary because of all the benefits and Graces obtained.
- Therefore, the person gets a hint by devotion to the Rosary. This is not to say that praying the Rosary guarantees salvation - by no means.
- In looking at promises #3 and #4 above, praying the Rosary helps one to live a holy life, which is itself a great sign that a soul is on the road to salvation.

"Who hath predestinated us unto the adoption of children through Jesus Christ unto himself: according to the purpose of his will: Unto the praise of the glory of his grace, in which he hath graced us in his beloved son. In whom we also are called by lot, being predestinated according to the purpose of him who worketh all things according to the counsel of his will." -Ephesians 1:5-6,11-12

History Of The Rosary

Within the early history of the Rosary, only 100 years later, devotion to the Rosary declined substantially. Not long after the Black Plague swept across Europe in the 1300s, Mary choose Blessed Alan de la Roche to re-establish devotion to her Rosary.

The people needed the peace and reassurance that this prayer brings more than ever.

Alan belonged to the order St. Dominic founded. He was a Dominican preacher from Brittany. In 1460 Alan was visited by Jesus.

Jesus gave him a warning:

"How can you crucify Me again so soon?" Jesus questioned Alan. "You crucified Me once before by your sins and I would willingly be crucified again rather than have My Father offended by the sins you used to commit. You are crucifying Me again now because you have all the learning and understanding that you need to preach My Mother's Rosary, and you are not doing so. If you only did this you could teach many souls that right path and lead them away from sin - but you are not doing it and so, you yourself are guilty of the sins that they commit."

These unforgettable words from Jesus set Alan afire and he went out with as much fervor as St. Dominic himself had and preached the Rosary.

Mary also appeared to Alan. She also had a message for him: *"You were a great sinner in your youth but I obtained the grace of your conversion from my Son. Had such a thing been possible I would have liked to have gone through all kinds of suffering to save you because converted sinners are a glory to me. And I would have done this also to make you worthy of preaching my Rosary far and wide."*

Alan was visited not only by Jesus and Mary but also St. Dominic, the father of his order and the original preacher of the Rosary. St. Dominic mentored Alan. One of the things he told Alan was, *"See the wonderful results I have had through preaching the Holy Rosary! You and all those who love Our Lady ought to do the same so that, by means of this holy practice of the Rosary, you may draw all people to the real science of the virtues."*

The Rosary is the best way to honor the mother of Jesus. It brings peace to peoples lives by bringing them closer to Jesus. This prayer is so pleasing to Jesus that He will not allow people to forget its saving powers.

In 1521, Alberto da Castello, another Dominican Preacher created a book called The Rosary of the Glorious Virgin Mary. This publication is the first time the Rosary appeared in the form that it is prayed today.

Adding to the history of the rosary, another Dominican Preacher made a standard form for the Rosary. Pope St. Pius V did this at the time of the famous Battle of Lepanto in the mid-1500s.

History Of The Rosary: What Do Modern Popes Have To Say About The Rosary?

Pope Pius IX - Reign 1846-1878

- *"Among all the devotions approved by the Church none has been favored by so many miracles as the devotion of the Most Holy Rosary."*
- *"We do not wish here to pass over in silence the fact that the Blessed Virgin herself, even in our times has solicitously recommended this manner of prayer, when she appeared and taught it to the innocent girl in the Grotto of Lourdes."*

Pope Leo XIII - Reign 1878-1903

"A powerful means of renewing our courage will undoubtedly be found in the Holy Rosary."

Pope Benedict XV - Reign 1914-1922

"This prayer is perfect because of the praise it offers because of the lessons it imparts because of the graces it obtains and because of the triumphs it achieves."

Pope Pius XI - Reign 1922-1939

- *"If you desire peace in your hearts, your homes and your country, assemble every evening to recite the Rosary."*
- *"Among the various supplications with which we successfully appeal to the Virgin Mother of God, the Holy Rosary*

without doubt occupies a special and distinct place."

- *"Tell your faithful people that the Pope is not satisfied with simply blessing the Rosary, but that he prays his Rosary everyday and invites all his children to do the same."*

Pope Pius XII - Reign 1939-1958

- *"There is no surer means of calling down God's blessings upon the family ... than the daily recitation of the Rosary."*
- *"We do not hesitate to affirm again publicly that we put great confidence in the Holy Rosary for the healing of evils which afflict our times."*

Pope John Paul II - Reign 1978-2005

- *"Yet the Rosary clearly belongs to the kind of veneration of the Mother of God described by the Council: a devotion directed to the Christological center of the Christian faith, in such a way that when the Mother is honored, the Son ... is duly known, loved and glorified,"*
- *"If properly revitalized, the Rosary is an aid and certainly not a hindrance to ecumenism!"*
- *"The Rosary represents a most effective means of fostering among the faithful that*

commitment to the contemplation of the Christian mystery."

Pope Benedict XVI - Reign 2005-present

- *"Today, together we confirm that the Holy Rosary is not a pious practice banished to the past. Instead, the Rosary is experiencing a new Springtime."*
- *"In the current world ... this prayer helps to put Christ at the center, as the Virgin did, who meditated within all that was said about her Son, and also what he did and said."*
- *"The Rosary, when it is prayed in an authentic way... brings, in fact, peace and reconciliation*

Origin Of The Rosary: Where Does The Rosary Get Its Name?

The Rosary may at first seem complicated and difficult to incorporate into one's quotidian life, but its value is immense and mysterious. This book serves as a reminder of such mysterious benefits, encouraging with stories and testimonies of the power of the Rosary, and also functioning as a practical guide and prayer map in how to pray the Rosary.

There is a story that has been passed down in history about St. Domenic (b. 1170 – d. 1221) and a holy woman who, despite St. Dominic's command, would not pray the Rosary. This story is recorded by St.

Louis de Montfort (b. 1673 d. 1716) in a text titled The Secret Life of the Rosary:

Whatever you do, do not be like a certain pious but stubborn lady in Rome, so often mentioned when speaking about the Rosary. She was so devout and so fervent that she put to shame by her holy life even the strictest religious in the Church. Having decided to ask Saint Dominic's advice about her spiritual life, she asked him to hear her confession.

For penance he gave her one whole Rosary to say and advised her to say it every day. She said that she had no time to say it, excusing herself on the grounds that she made the Stations of Rome every day, that she wore sackcloth and a hair shirt, that she carried out so many other penances and fasted so much.

Saint Dominic urged her repeatedly to take his advice and say the Rosary, but she would not hear of it. She left the confessional, horrified at the tactics of this new spiritual director who had tried so hard to persuade her to take on a devotion that was not at all to her liking.

Later on, when she was in prayer, she fell into ecstasy and had a vision of her soul appearing before Our Lord's Judgment Seat. Saint Michael put all her penances and other prayers onto one tray of the scales and all her sins and imperfections onto the other tray. The tray of her good works was greatly outweighed by the tray with her sins and imperfections. Filled with terror she cried for mercy, imploring the Blessed

Virgin Mary's help. Her gracious Advocate took the one and only Rosary that she had said for her penance and dropped it onto the tray of her good works. This one Rosary was so heavy that it weighed more than all her sins as well as all her good works. Our Lady then reproved her for refusing to follow the counsel of her servant Dominic and for not saying the Rosary every day. As soon as she came to she rushed and threw herself at Saint Dominic's feet, and told him all that had happened. She begged his forgiveness for her unbelief and promised to say the Rosary faithfully every day. By this means, she arose to Christian perfection and finally to the glory of everlasting life.

You who are people of prayer— learn from this how tremendous is the power, the value and the importance of this devotion of the Most Holy Rosary when it is said together with meditation on the mysteries.

The origin of the rosary has a rich history that continues to bring peace to peoples lives.

The word rosary itself comes from the Latin word rosarium, which means rose garden or garland of roses.

When you pray the Rosary it is like taking a peaceful walk through Mary's rose garden. A garden filled with beautiful, fragrant roses. There are:

- *White roses:* that tell the joys of a child and His mother

- *Yellow roses:* that speak the truth of a Teacher and His first believer
- *Red roses:* that tell of the sorrows of a Man and a woman
- *Golden roses:* that tell the glories of a King and a queen

The Origin of the rosary is so rich with history, yet all the mysteries can be applied to your every day, modern situations. It has deep roots, yet is still enduring even in this hectic age.

Power Of The Rosary Proves: That You Can Find Peace By Praying This Catholic Prayer

"It's so good to know that I have such a powerful weapon like the rosary, to help me in all my trials."

The power of the Rosary was immediately demonstrated during St. Dominic's time and continues to be seen today. Not only will the Rosary bring peace to your personal life, but it is also a powerful tool that can bring peace to the entire world.

Sr. Lucia, one of the children Mary appeared to at Fatima, stated in a 1957 interview:

"The Most Holy Virgin, in these last times in which we live, has given new efficacy in the recitation of the Holy Rosary".

"She has given this efficacy to such an extent that there is no problem, no matter how difficult it is, whether temporal or above all spiritual, in families, of the families in the world, or of the religious communities, or even of the life of peoples and nations, that cannot be solved by the Rosary".

"There is no problem, I tell you, no matter how difficult it is, that we cannot solve by the prayer of the Holy Rosary. With the Holy Rosary, we will save ourselves. We will sanctify ourselves. We will console Our Lord and obtain the salvation of many souls."

The truth in Sr. Lucia's words and the power of the Rosary are clearly demonstrated as you read the following historical events:

- Awesome power of the Rosary demonstrated through military victories
- Special defense of the Catholic Church
- Powerful instrument for conversion and victory over vice
- Favorite method of honoring the mother of Jesus
- Even non-Catholic Christians pray the Rosary

As you learn of this powerful weapon against Satan, you will begin to see the importance of honoring

Mary by making a habit of praying the Rosary everyday.

Mary's intercessory power is strong before the throne of God because Jesus would deny His Mother nothing.

And, like any good mother, Mary wants to help her dear children on earth.

The daily recitation of the Rosary will work wonders in your personal life teaching you the way to holiness and peace.

Honoring Mary by praying the Rosary will attain peace in the world and will keep the Church safe from her enemies.

Pray the Rosary everyday!

CHAPTER 3
ROSARY PRAYERS

Who Can Pray the Rosary

Anyone who knows six easy prayers can pray a Rosary; you will also need to know twenty Mysteries to meditate upon as you pray. You do not have to be a Catholic.

The Order of Prayers

The Rosary begins with the Apostles Creed, followed by one Our Father, three Hail Marys (traditionally offered for an increase in faith, hope, and charity for those praying the Rosary), a Glory Be, and, if desired, the Fatima Prayer. Next come five mysteries, each consisting of one Our Father, ten Hail Marys, a Glory Be, and, if desired, the Fatima Prayers. Conclude with the Hail Holy Queen. Please say a few extra prayers after the Hail Holy Queen for the Pope.

Rosary Beads

If you do not have Rosary beads, it is perfectly okay to count with your fingers. Counting beads frees your mind to help you meditate.

The Prayers of the Rosary

These prayers are intermittently necessary in the praying of the mysteries and thus it is best to, not only be familiar with them, but also keep them as a point of reference and bedrock when praying the holy Rosary.

The Apostles' Creed

I believe in God,

the Father almighty,

Creator of heaven and earth,

and in Jesus Christ, his only Son, our Lord,

who was conceived by the Holy Spirit,

born of the Virgin Mary,

suffered under Pontius Pilate,

was crucified, died, and was buried;

he descended into hell;

on the third day he rose again from the dead;

he ascended into heaven,

and is seated at the right hand of God the Father almighty;

from there he will come to judge the living and the dead.

I believe in the Holy Spirit,

the holy catholic Church,

the communion of saints,

the forgiveness of sins,

the resurrection of the body,

and life everlasting.

Amen.

The Our Father

Our father, who art in heaven,

hallowed be thy name;

thy kingdom come;

thy will be done on earth as it is in heaven.

Give us this day our daily bread;

and forgive us our trespasses

as we forgive those who trespass

against us;

and lead us not into temptation,

but deliver us from evil.

Amen.

 The Hail Mary

Hail Mary, full of grace, the Lord is with you;

blessed are you among women,

and blessed is the fruit of your womb, Jesus.

Holy Mary, Mother of God,

pray for us sinners now and at the hour of our death.

Amen.

The Glory Be (The Doxology)

Glory be to the Father, the Son, and the Holy Spirit;

as it was in the beginning, is now, and ever shall be,

world without end.

Amen.

The Hail Holy Queen (The Salve Regina)

Hail, holy Queen, mother of mercy,

our life, our sweetness, and our hope.

To you we cry, poor banished children of Eve;

to you we send up our sighs,

mourning, and weeping in this valley of tears.

Turn, then, most gracious advocate,

your eyes of mercy toward us;

and after this, our exile,

show unto us the blessed fruit of your womb, Jesus.

O clement, O loving, O sweet Virgin Mary.

HOW TO PRAY IN ROSARY

Devout Christians may amass quite a collection of rosaries — from simple plastic rosaries to more ornate gem-enhanced alternatives — and never really put them to use. But reciting the rosary is an important way for Christians to express their faith, and families can make such expressions by reciting the rosary together.

The United States Conference of Catholic Bishops says the rosary is a scripture-based prayer that begins with the "Apostles' Creed," continues with the "Our Father," and then the "Hail Mary." "Glory Be" is prayed at the end. The first prayer summarizes the great mysteries of the Catholic faith. Praying the "Our father" introduces each mystery from the Biblical Gospels. Finally, the "Hail Mary" announces the birth of Christ.

In addition to the prayers, saying the rosary includes announcing the Divine Mysteries of Contemplation, usually prayed on particular days of the week. These include the Joyful Mysteries (Mondays and Saturdays), Sorrowful mysteries (Tuesdays and Fridays), Glorious mysteries (Wednesdays and Sundays) and Luminous mysteries (Thursdays). There are five mysteries for each category.

When getting started, you may not be familiar with the rosary. But with practice, you soon will have the repetition of prayers set to memory.

In order to pray the rosary, it is helpful to use rosary beads to count one's prayers so as not to be distracted by counting.

1. Make the sign of the cross on the crucifix, then pray the Apostle's Creed:

I believe in God, the Father Almighty, Creator of Heaven and earth; and in Jesus Christ, His only Son, Our Lord, Who was conceived by the Holy Ghost, born of the Virgin Mary, suffered under Pontius Pilate, was crucified; died, and was buried. He descended into Hell; the third day He arose again from the dead; He ascended into Heaven, sitteth at the right hand of God, the Father Almighty; from thence He shall come to judge the living and the dead. I believe in the Holy Spirit, the holy Catholic Church, the communion of saints, the forgiveness of sins, the resurrection of the body, and life everlasting. Amen

2. Then, on the next large bead, say the Our father:

Our Father, Who art in heaven, hallowed be Thy name; Thy kingdom come; Thy will be done on earth as it is in heaven. Give us this day our daily bread; and forgive us our trespasses as we forgive those who trespass against us; and lead us not into temptation, but deliver us from evil, Amen.

3. With fingers on the next three small beads, pray three Hail Marys:

Hail Mary, full of grace. The Lord is with thee. Blessed art thou among women, and blessed is the fruit of thy womb, Jesus. Holy Mary, Mother of God, pray for us sinners, now and at the hour of our death. Amen.

4. On the chain, pray the Glory Be:

Glory be to the Father, to the Son, and to the Holy Spirit, as it was, is now, and ever shall be, world without end. Amen.

5. On the large bead, meditate on the first mystery and pray the Our Father (again):

Our father, Who art in heaven, hallowed be Thy name; Thy kingdom come; Thy will be done on earth as it is in heaven. Give us this day our daily bread; and forgive us our trespasses as we forgive those who trespass against us; and lead us not into temptation, but deliver us from evil, Amen.

6. One must pray mysteries based on each of the five sections (or decades) of the rosary depending on the day of the week:

MONDAYS AND SATURDAYS

The Joyful Mysteries remind the faithful of Christ's birth:

- The Annunciation (Luke 1:26–38); The Visitation (Luke 1:39–56)
- The Nativity (Luke 2:1–21)
- The Presentation (Luke 2:22–38)
- The Finding of the Child Jesus in the Temple (Luke 2:41–52)
- Tuesdays and Fridays

The Sorrowful Mysteries recall Jesus' passion and death:

- The Agony of Jesus in the Garden (Matthew 26:36–56)
- The Scourging at the Pillar (Matthew 27:26)
- The Crowning with Thorns (Matthew 27:27–31)
- The Carrying of the Cross (Matthew 27:32)
- The Crucifixion (Matthew 27:33–56).
- Wednesdays and Sundays

The Glorious Mysteries focus on the resurrection of Jesus and the glories of heaven:

- The Resurrection (John 20:1–29)
- The Ascension (Luke 24:36–53)
- The Descent of the Holy Spirit (Acts 2:1–41)
- The Assumption of Mary, the Mother of God, into heaven; The Coronation of Mary in heaven.
- Thursdays

The Mysteries of Light, also known as the Luminous Mysteries, in 2002:

- The Baptism in the River Jordan (Matthew 3:13–16)
- The Wedding Feast at Cana (John 2:1–11)
- The Preaching of the coming of the Kingdom of God (Mark 1:14–15)
- The Transfiguration (Matthew 17:1–8)
- The Institution of the Holy Eucharist (Matthew 26).

7. One must repeat Steps 5 and 6 four additional times in order to complete the next four decades.

8. At the end of your Rosary, say the Hail Holy Queen:

Hail, Holy Queen, Mother of mercy, our life, our sweetness, and our hope. To thee do we cry, poor banished children of Eve, to thee do we send up our sighs, mourning and weeping in this valley of tears. Turn then, most gracious advocate, thine eyes of mercy toward us; and after this our exile show unto us the blessed fruit of thy womb Jesus, O clement, O loving, O sweet Virgin Mary.

Pray for us, O holy Mother of God. That we may be made worthy of the promises of Christ.

O God, whose only-begotten Son, by His life, death, and resurrection, has purchased for us the rewards of eternal salvation; grant we beseech Thee, that meditating upon these mysteries of the most holy Rosary of the Blessed Virgin Mary, we may imitate what they contain and obtain what they promise. Through the same Christ our Lord. Amen.

9. Finally, make the "Sign of the Cross."

Suggestion: Pope Saint John Paul II advises the prayer of the Rosary as follows: the Joyful mysteries said on Monday and Saturday; the Luminous on Thursday; the Sorrowful on Tuesday and Friday; and the Glorious on Wednesday and Sunday

A Practical Guide on How to Pray the Rosary

The effects of the Rosary are not immediate. The mysteries and miracles do not usually occur overnight. However, with an attitude of discipline and consistency, one can surely arrive at a life full of purpose and dedication if one chooses to commit to the Rosary. But first, it must become a normal and regular part of your personal prayer life. This doesn't necessarily mean you must pray it every day. You can choose to pray it every Wednesday night, or maybe the first Friday of every month. The most significant part of the prayer is simply making a commitment.

St. Anthony Mary Claret once said, "When people love and recite the rosary they find it makes them better."

es pertaining to the life of Jesus? One might reply that the Christianity can be rooted in Jesus, thus all component must relate to him. Mary is viewed as a means to Jesus and her importance within the rosary possesses decreased significantly since its initial creation.

Another concern to be raised is the fact that the Catholic Church prides itself on its traditions. The roots of the Rosary relate to the 150 Psalms included within the Bible, the modern rosary seems to have no relation to that whatsoever. The response to this may simply be related to the actual fact that the rosary is an informal practice and has got adapted through period. The mysteries of the rosary take up a larger role when compared to the Psalms.

Though the history of beads serves as a useful approach to counting, Catholicism has got adapted its utility If you commit your life to praying the Rosary, you will arrive at a correct and true perspective, bettering yourself and reminding yourself of the purpose of life.

The Rosary has a body and a soul, and the body of the Rosary is made up of the prayers. Some of those prayers come in groups of ten, called a "decade." The

Rosary allows us to meditate on the twenty important events in the life and teachings of Jesus as well as his mother, Mary—these events make up the Rosary's spirit and soul, and are referred to as the Mysteries. As we pray the Mysteries, we must think about how the biblical stories apply to our quotidian lives — because here is where lies the Rosary's transforming power.

"The Rosary... floods the should of those who recite it devoutly with an ever new sweetness of piety, giving them the impression and emotion as if they were hearing the very voice of their most merciful Mother explaining these mysteries to them, and conversing with them at length for their salvation..." is how Pope Leo XIII described the Rosary over a hundred years ago.

Personal prayer separated the Catholic rosary from other types of popular devotion, because, even when one does not having a bead string, one's fingertips can easily serve as a subsitute and reminder that while meditating the whole body and mind should be focused on the mysteries. The power in repetition is engraves the truth into one's mind, thus rendering application easier.

Though the practice of the rosary shows up repetitive naturally, it is important to look at the big picture. The ritual is said to be a way of prayer offered to Mary. Why then are the mysteriinto a practice and object offering far greater program to practitioners within the faith. The rosary as talked about earlier plays a vital role in ways of devotion to both Jesus and Mary. The physical beads of the rosary serve as a practical counter during prayers. The actual tailor made of praying the rosary is completed to be able to build a stronger relationship with God or even to be pious.

CHAPTER 4
ROSARY MYSTERIES

THE TWENTY MYSTERIES

Here is a brief listing and description of all twenty Mysteries:

1. The Joyful Mysteries

- The Annunciation: The Archangel Gabriel "announces" to Mary that she shall conceive the Son of God.
- The Visitation: Mary visits her cousin Elizabeth, who is pregnant with John the Baptist.
- The Nativity: Jesus is born.
- The Presentation: Mary and Joseph "present" Jesus in the Temple where they meet Simeon.
- The Finding in the Temple: After losing Him, Mary and Joseph find young Jesus teaching the Rabbis in the Temple.

2. The Luminous Mysteries

- The Baptism in the Jordan: The voice of the Father declares Jesus the beloved Son.
- The Wedding at Cana: Christ changes water into wine, his first public miracle.

- The Proclamation of the Kingdom: Jesus calls to conversion (cf. Mk 1:15) and forgives the sins of all who draw near to him.
- The Transfiguration: The glory of the Godhead shines forth from the face of Christ.
- The Institution of the Eucharist: Jesus offers the first Mass at the Last Supper with his apostles, establishing the sacramental foundation for all Christian living.

3. The Sorrowful Mysteries

- The Agony in the Garden: Jesus sweats water and blood while praying the night before his passion.
- The Scourging at the Pillar: Pilate has Jesus whipped.
- The Crowning with Thorns: Roman soldiers crown Jesus' head with thorns.
- The Carrying of the Cross: Jesus meets His mother and falls three times on the way up Calvary.
- The Crucifixion: Jesus is nailed to the cross and dies before His mother and His apostle John.

4. The Glorious Mysteries

- The Resurrection: Jesus rises from the dead.

- The Ascension: Jesus leaves the Apostles and bodily "ascends" to heaven.
- The Descent of the Holy Spirit: The Apostles receive the Holy Spirit in tongues of fire in the upper room with Mary.
- The Assumption: Mary is taken bodily--assumed--into heaven by God at the end of her life here on earth.
- The Coronation: Mary is crowned Queen of Heaven and Earth.

THE JOYFUL MYSTERIES

The Joyful Mysteries are said on Monday and Saturday (during the season of Advent they are recited on Sundays).

The are made up of:

- The Annunciation
- The Visitation
- The Nativity
- The Presentation
- The Finding of Jesus in the Temple.

After easy Joyful Mystery, one must say the *"Fatima Prayer,"* which is:

O my Jesus, forgive our sins,
Save us from the fire of hell,
Lead all souls to Heaven,
Especially those who are in most need of Thy Mercy.

After completing a group of five Mysteries, one must say the Hail Holy Queen prayer.

The Annunciation

The angel Gabriel was sent from God to a town of Galilee called Nazareth, to a virgin betrothed to a man named Joseph, of the house of David, and the virgin's name was Mary. And coming to her, he said, "Hail, favored one! The Lord is with you." But she was greatly troubled at what was said and pondered what sort of greeting this might be. Then, the angel, said to her, "Do not be afraid, Mary, for you have found favor with God. Behold, you will conceive in your womb and bear a son, and you shall name him Jesus. He will be great and will be called Son of the Most High, and the Lord God will give him the throne of David his father, and he will rule over the house of Jacob forever, and of his kingdom, there will be no end." Mary said, *"Behold, I am the handmaid of the Lord. May it be done to me according to your word."* Then the angel departed from her. (Luke 1:26-33, 38)

As an angel proclaimed the conception of Christ in Mary's virginal womb, so do mothers and fathers learn every day of the conception of their child. Let us pray to the Mother of all the Living that every child be treasured and protected from the first moment of conception as an inestimable and wondrous gift of God.

Our Father...

Holy Mary, Mother of Joy: inspire the hearts of all newly pregnant women with the joy of which you sang at the Annunciation.

Hail Mary, full of grace...

Holy Mary, Mother of Joy: deliver all parents from fear, and implant in their hearts a joyful hope...

Hail Mary, full of grace...

Holy Mary, Mother of Joy: pray that joy may embrace the lives of all expectant parents...

Hail Mary, full of grace...

Holy Mary, Mother of Joy: pray for grandparents, that the witness of their joy might be a source of strength to their expectant children...

Hail Mary, full of grace...

Holy Mary, Mother of Joy: be with all new parents, that the miracle of new life silently growing in the womb will awaken in them a commitment to cherish and protect their child...

Hail Mary, full of grace...

Holy Mary, Mother of Joy: pray that all might be inspired by the wonder of new life and embrace God's overwhelming gift...

Hail Mary, full of grace...

Holy Mary, Mother of Joy: watch over all new parents with your maternal care, from the first moments of new life...

Hail Mary, full of grace...

Holy Mary, Mother of Joy: rejoice with the mother who first feels the stirring of the child in her womb...

Hail Mary, full of grace...

Holy Mary, Mother of Joy: intercede for all parents who long to carry a child in their arms...

Hail Mary, full of grace...

Holy Mary, Mother of Joy: Bless adoptive parents and rejoice with them in the beauty of their child...

Hail Mary, full of grace...

Glory to the Father, and to the Son, and to the Holy Spirit:

As it was in the beginning, is now, and will be for ever. Amen.

Fruit of the Mystery: Humility

The Visitation

During those days Mary set out and traveled to the hill country in haste to a town of Judah, where she entered the house of Zechariah and greeted Elizabeth. When Elizabeth heard Mary's greeting, the infant leaped in her womb, and Elizabeth, filled with the holy Spirit, cried out in a loud voice and said, "Most blessed are you among women, and blessed is the fruit of your womb. And how does this happen to me, that the mother of my Lord should come to me? For at the moment the sound of your greeting reached my ears, the infant in my womb leaped for joy. Blessed are you who believed that what was spoken to you by the Lord would be fulfilled." (Luke 1:39-45)

As the child in Elizabeth's womb leaped for joy when the Blessed Virgin, pregnant with the Son of God, came to meet her, so may our hearts leap with joy at the wonders of new life promised in every expectant mother.

Our Father...

Holy Mary, Mother of Joy: Inspire us to rejoice with all expectant parents and to support them with our prayers...

Hail Mary, full of grace...

Holy Mary, Mother of Joy: Comfort expectant fathers when they are afraid...

Hail Mary, full of grace...

Holy Mary, Mother of Joy: Share your courage with all women who fear the coming birth of their child...

Hail Mary, full of grace...

Holy Mary, Mother of Joy: Be close to all expectant mothers, as they bear the child of their womb...

Hail Mary, full of grace...

Holy Mary, Mother of Joy: Give us the joy of Saint Elizabeth and her son whenever we meet the miracle of new life...

Hail Mary, full of grace ...

Holy Mary, Mother of Joy: Pray that all our laws may protect and defend the innocent life which lives within each mother's womb...

Hail Mary, full of grace...

Holy Mary, Mother of Joy: Give courage by your example to those who greet the news of their pregnancy with fear...

Hail Mary, full of grace...

Holy Mary, Mother of Joy: Teach us to support all expectant parents and to increase their joy in the miracle of God's work within them...

Hail Mary, full of grace...

Holy Mary, Mother of Joy: Ask that God gives us the wisdom to support those tempted to abort their child's life...

Hail Mary, full of grace...

Holy Mary, Mother of Joy: Inspire even those who perform abortions with the truth of him whom you bore in your womb...

Hail Mary, full of grace...

Glory to the Father, and to the Son, and to the Holy Spirit:

as it was in the beginning, is now, and will be for ever. Amen.

Fruit of the Mystery: Love of Neighbor

The Nativity

While they were there, the time came for her to have her child and she gave birth to her firstborn son. She wrapped him in swaddling clothes and laid him in a manger, because there was no room for them in the inn. Now there were shepherds in that region living in the fields and keeping the night watch over their flock. The angel of the Lord appeared to them and the glory of the Lord shone around them, and they were struck with great fear. The angel said to them,

"Do not be afraid; for behold, I proclaim to you good news of great joy that will be for all the people. For today in the city of David a savior has been born for you who is Messiah and Lord. And this will be a sign for you: you will find an infant wrapped in swaddling clothes and lying in a manger." (Luke 2: 6-12)

In the birth of every child we see the birth of Christ Jesus in the Bethlehem stable. Let us commend all new mothers and fathers and every newborn child to the protection and intercession of the Mother of God and Mother of all Christians.

Our Father...

Holy Mary, Mother of Joy: Come swiftly to the aid of all who labor in distress...

Hail Mary, full of grace...

Holy Mary, Mother of Joy: Give your own courage to mothers who are alone or abandoned...

Hail Mary, full of grace...

Holy Mary, Mother of Joy: Implant within the hearts of all grandparents the wonder known by the shepherds at the birth of your Son...

Hail Mary, full of grace...

Holy Mary, Mother of Joy: pray for those who assist with the labor which brings new life: for skill and compassion...

Hail Mary, full of grace...

Holy Mary, Mother of Joy: Help us to welcome the gift of new life, as you welcomed the birth of your Son...

Hail Mary, full of grace...

Holy Mary, Mother of Joy: Strengthen the joy of all men and women who behold the wonder of new life...

Hail Mary, full of grace...

Holy Mary, Mother of Joy: Let, the face of the newborn child, proclaim the Gospel of Life...

Hail Mary, full of grace...

Holy Mary, Mother of Joy: Guide the hands and hearts of obstetricians in their holy work...

Hail Mary, full of grace...

Holy Mary, Mother of Joy: help us to proclaim the Gospel of Life in our care for each newborn child...

Hail Mary, full of grace...

Holy Mary, Mother of Joy: be present at the moment of birth to share in our joy...

Hail Mary, full of grace...

Glory to the Father, and to the Son, and to the Holy Spirit: as it was in the beginning, is now, and will be forever. Amen.

Fruit of the Mystery: Poverty

The Presentation

Now there was a man in Jerusalem whose name was Simeon. This man was righteous and devout, awaiting the consolation of Israel, and the holy Spirit was upon him. It had been revealed to him by the holy Spirit that he should not see death before he had seen the Messiah of the Lord. He came in the Spirit into the temple; and when the parents brought in the child Jesus to perform the custom of the law in regard to him, he took him into his arms and blessed God, saying:

"Now, Master, you may let your servant go in peace, according to your word, for my eyes have seen your salvation, which you prepared in sight of all the peoples, a light for revelation to the Gentiles, and glory for your people Israel." (Luke 2:25-32)

As Christ was consecrated to God at his presentation in the temple, so many we consecrate all children to that holiness, purity, and innocence by which they lead us to God. "A little child shall lead them."

Our Father...

Holy Mary, Mother of Joy: watch over every child and keep them safe and close to your Son...

Hail Mary, full of grace...

Holy Mary, Mother of Joy: Inspire all mothers to care for their children, as you cared for the child Jesus...

Hail Mary, full of grace...

Holy Mary, Mother of Joy: Be with all fathers of newborn babies that they might glory in the wonder of new life...

Hail Mary, full of grace...

Holy Mary, Mother of Joy: Gently guide new parents as they lead their little ones to your Son...

Hail Mary, full of grace...

Holy Mary, Mother of Joy: Pray for the toddler who, like your Son, reaches out in hope to a brand new world...

Hail Mary, full of grace...

Holy Mary, Mother of Joy: Hold close to your immaculate heart the innocence and joy of each little child...

Hail Mary, full of grace...

Holy Mary, Mother of Joy: Be a model of maternal love for those who need you the most...

Hail Mary, full of grace...

Holy Mary, Mother of Joy: Bless with your presence the room of each little child...

Hail Mary, full of grace ...

Holy Mary, Mother of Joy: Welcome home to heaven the soul of the miscarried child...

Hail Mary, full of grace...

Holy Mary, Mother of Joy: Rejoice with us, as you did with Saint Joseph, at the first steps and first words of every child...

Hail Mary, full of grace...

Glory to the Father, and to the Son, and to the Holy Spirit:

As it was in the beginning, is now, and will be forever. Amen.

Fruit of the Mystery: Obedience

The Finding of Jesus in the Temple

Each year his parents went to Jerusalem for the feast of Passover, and when he was twelve years old, they went up according to festival custom. After they had completed its days, as they were returning, the boy Jesus remained behind in Jerusalem, but his parents did not know it. Thinking that he was in the caravan, they journeyed for a day and looked for him among their relatives and acquaintances, but not finding him, they returned to Jerusalem to look for him. After three days they found him in the temple, sitting in the midst of the teachers, listening to them and asking them questions, and all who heard him were astounded at his understanding and his answers. When his parents saw him, they were astonished, and his mother said to him,

"Son, why have you done this to us? Your father and I have been looking for you with great anxiety." And he said to them, "Why were you looking for me? Did you not know that I must be in my Father's house?" But they did not understand what he said to them. (Luke 2:41-50)

As the Christ Child was found in the temple by the Blessed Virgin Mary and Saint Joseph, so we pray for all children, especially those lost and forgotten. May the Gospel of Life impel us to find them when they are most in need and to lead them home to a place where they are treasured, protected, and loved.

Our Father...

Holy Mary, Mother of Joy: Bring joy to the lives of children who are abused in body or mind...

Hail Mary, full of grace...

Holy Mary, Mother of Joy: Deliver the abusive adult from the evil of their actions...

Hail Mary, full of grace...

Holy Mary, Mother of Joy: Guide those who work to find children who are lost...

Hail Mary, full of grace...

Holy Mary, Mother of Joy: Pray for all children unwanted or abandoned, and lead them home...

Hail Mary, full of grace...

Holy Mary, Mother of Joy: Be with parents unable to care for their children: teach them patience and holiness...

Hail Mary, full of grace...

Holy Mary, Mother of Joy: Teach young parents to treasure their child as you loved the Child Jesus...

Hail Mary, full of grace...

Holy Mary, Mother of Joy: Pray for doctors who have abandoned the practice of the faith: lead them home to your Son...

Hail Mary, full of grace...

Holy Mary, Mother of Joy: Intercede with your son for all who perform abortions that they may be freed from a blindness to the evil of their actions...

Hail Mary, full of grace...

Holy Mary, Mother of Joy: Inspire all legislators by your love for us, that they might work for the protection of life...

Hail Mary, full of grace...

Holy Mary, Mother of Joy: Guide, by your holy example, all who seek to lead us and lead them to a love for the Gospel of Life...

Hail Mary, full of grace...

Glory to the Father, and to the Son, and to the Holy Spirit:

as it was in the beginning, is now, and will be forever. Amen.

Fruit of the Mystery: Joy in Finding Jesus

THE LUMINOUS MYSTERIES

The Luminous Mysteries are made up of The Baptism in the Jordan, The Wedding at Cana, The Proclamation of the Kingdom of God, The Transfiguration, and The Institution of the Eucharist.

The Baptism in the Jordan

Jesus begins his public ministry being baptized by John.

Our Father . . .

For our sake he made him to be sin who did not know sin, so that we might become the righteousness of God in him. 2 Cor 5:21

Hail Mary . . .

He went throughout (the) whole region of the Jordan, proclaiming a baptism of repentance for the forgiveness of sins, as it is written in . . . Isaiah: "A voice of one crying out in the desert: 'Prepare the way of the Lord, make straight his paths.'" Lk 3:3

Hail Mary . . .

And the crowds asked him, "What then should we do?" He said to them in reply, "Whoever has two cloaks should share with the person who has none. And whoever has food should do likewise." Lk 3:10-11

Hail Mary . . .

Jesus also had been baptized . . . heaven was opened and the holy Spirit descended upon him in bodily form like a dove. And a voice came from heaven, "You are my beloved Son; with you I am well pleased." Lk 3:21-22

Hail Mary . . .

Here is my servant whom I uphold, / my chosen one with whom I am pleased, / Upon whom I have put my spirit. Is 42:1

Hail Mary . . .

A bruised reed he shall not break, / and a smoldering wick he shall not quench. Is 42:3

Hail Mary . . .

I, the LORD, have called you for the victory of justice. Is 42:6

Hail Mary . . .

I formed you, and set you / as a covenant of the people, / a light for the nations. Is 42:6

Hail Mary . . .

"The Spirit of the Lord is upon me, / because he has anointed me / to bring glad tidings to the poor." Lk 4:18

Hail Mary . . .

"He has sent me to proclaim liberty to captives / and recovery of sight to the blind, / to let the oppressed go free, / and to proclaim a year acceptable to the Lord." Lk 4:18-19

Hail Mary . . .

Glory be . . .

LORD JESUS, HELP US TO PERSEVERE

IN LIVING OUT OUR BAPTISMAL PROMISES.

The Wedding at Cana

Jesus performs his first public sign revealing his true identity, at the request of his mother.

Our Father . . .

When the wine ran short, the mother of Jesus said to him, "They have no wine." Jn 2:3

Hail Mary . . .

Jesus said to her, "Woman, how does your concern affect me? My hour has not yet come." Jn 2:4

Hail Mary . . .

His mother said to the servers, "Do whatever he tells you." Jn 2:5

Hail Mary . . .

Jesus told them, "Fill the jars with water." So they filled them to the brim. Then he told them, "Draw some out now and take it to the headwaiter." Jn 2:7-8

Hail Mary . . .

The headwaiter called the bridegroom and said to him, "Everyone serves good wine first, and then when people have drunk freely, an inferior one; but you have kept the good wine until now." Jn 2:9-10

Hail Mary . . .

If I . . . have washed your feet, you ought to wash one another's feet. I have given you a model to follow, so that as I have done for you, you should also do. Jn 13:14-15

Hail Mary . . .

To you who hear I say, love your enemies, do good to those who hate you, bless those who curse you, pray for those who mistreat you. Lk 6:27-28

Hail Mary . . .

Stop judging and you will not be judged. Stop condemning and you will not be condemned. Forgive and you will be forgiven. Lk 6:37

Hail Mary . . .

Then he said to all, "If anyone wishes to come after me, he must deny himself and take up his cross daily and follow me." Lk 9:23

Hail Mary . . .

This is my commandment: love one another as I love you. Jn 15:12

Hail Mary . . .

Glory be . . .

LORD JESUS, OPEN US TO THE POWER OF YOUR

GRACE TO CHANGE OUR HEARTS AND LIVES.

The Proclamation of the Kingdom of God

After John was arrested, Jesus began proclaiming the Good News of God's kingdom.

Our father . . .

Jesus came to Galilee proclaiming the gospel of God. Mk 1:14

Hail Mary . . .

This is the time of fulfillment. The kingdom of God is at hand. Repent, and believe in the gospel. Mk 1:15

Hail Mary . . .

The Spirit of the Lord is upon me, / because he has anointed me / to bring glad tidings to the poor. Lk 4:18

Hail Mary . . .

He has sent me to proclaim liberty to captives / and recovery of sight to the blind, / to let the oppressed go free, / and to proclaim a year acceptable to the Lord. Lk 4:18-19

Hail Mary . . .

Today this scripture passage is fulfilled in your hearing. Lk 4:21

Hail Mary . . .

You have heard that it was said, "An eye for an eye and a tooth for a tooth." But I say to you . . . When someone strikes you on [your] right cheek, turn the other one to him as well. Mt 5:38-39

Hail Mary . . .

You have heard that it was said, "You shall love your neighbor and hate your enemy." But I say to you, love your enemies, and pray for those who persecute you. Mt 5:43-44

Hail Mary . . .

Do not store up for yourselves treasures on earth . . . But store up treasures in heaven . . . for where your treasure is, there also will your heart be. Mt 6:19-21

Hail Mary . . .

Do to others whatever you would have them do to you. This is the law and the prophets. Mt 7:12

Hail Mary . . .

Without cost you have received; without cost, you are to give. Mt 10:8

Hail Mary . . .

Glory be . . .

LORD JESUS, FILL US WITH THE DESIRE TO STRIVE FOR ONGOING CONVERSION.

The Transfiguration

Jesus is seen with Moses and Elijah, confirming that his suffering will end in glory.

Our Father . . .

Jesus took Peter, James, and John his brother, and led them up a high mountain by themselves. And he was transfigured before them; his face shone like the sun and his clothes became white as light. Mt 17:1-2

Hail Mary . . .

Two men were conversing with him, Moses and Elijah, who appeared in glory and spoke of his exodus that he was going to accomplish in Jerusalem. Lk 9:30-31

Hail Mary . . .

Peter and his companions . . . saw his glory and the two men standing with him. Lk 9:32

Hail Mary . . .

Peter said . . . "Master, it is good that we are here; let us make three tents. . . ." But he did not know what he was saying. Lk 9:33

Hail Mary . . .

A voice [said], "This is my beloved Son, with whom I am well pleased; listen to him." Mt 17:5

Hail Mary . . .

But Jesus came and touched them, saying, "Rise, and do not be afraid." And when the disciples raised their eyes, they saw no one else but Jesus alone. Mt 17:7-8

Hail Mary . . .

Through him was life, and this life was the light of the human race; the light shines in the darkness, and the darkness has not overcome it. Jn 1:4-5

Hail Mary . . .

No one has ever seen God. The only Son, God, who is at the Father's side, has revealed him. Jn 1:18

Hail Mary . . .

All of us, gazing with unveiled face on the glory of the Lord, are being transformed into the same image from glory to glory, as from the Lord who is the Spirit. 2 Cor 3:18

Hail Mary . . .

You are the light of the world . . . your light must shine before others, that they may see your good deeds and glorify your heavenly Father. Mt 5:14, 16

Hail Mary . . .

Glory be . . .

LORD JESUS, GRANT US THE COURAGE TO SHINE YOUR LIGHT IN OUR LIVES.

The Institution of the Eucharist.

At the last supper, Jesus instructs us to remember him in celebration of the Eucharist.

Our Father . . .

Before the feast of Passover, Jesus knew that his hour had come to pass from this world to the Father. He loved his own in the world and he loved them to the end. Jn 13:1

Hail Mary . . .

My appointed time draws near; in your house, I shall celebrate the Passover with my disciples. Mt 26:18

Hail Mary . . .

I have eagerly desired to eat this Passover with you before I suffer, for, I tell you, I shall not eat it [again] until there is fulfillment in the kingdom of God. Lk 22:15-16

Hail Mary . . .

Then he took the bread, said the blessing, broke it, and gave it to them, saying, "This is my body, which will be given for you; do this in memory of me." Lk 22:19

Hail Mary . . .

And likewise the cup after they had eaten, saying, "This cup is the new covenant in my blood, which will be shed for you." Lk 22:20

Hail Mary . . .

For as often as you eat this bread and drink the cup, you proclaim the death of the Lord until he comes. 1 Cor 11:26

Hail Mary . . .

I pray not only for them, but also for those who will believe in me through their word, so that they may all be one . . . that the world may believe that you sent me. Jn 17:20-21

Hail Mary . . .

Now you are Christ's body, and individually parts of it. 1 Cor 12:27

Hail Mary . . .

For in one Spirit we were all baptized into one body, whether Jews or Greeks, slaves or free persons, and we were all given to drink of one Spirit. 1 Cor 12:13

Hail Mary . . .

If [one] part suffers, all the parts suffer with it; if one part is honored, all the parts share its joy. 1 Cor 12:26

Hail Mary . . .

Glory be . . .

LORD JESUS, MAKE OF US A SIGN OF THE

UNITY FOR WHICH YOU PRAYED.

THE SORROWFUL MYSTERIES

The Five Sorrowful Mysteries are recited on the Tuesdays, Fridays, and Sundays of Lent. They are:

- The Agony in the Garden
- The Scourging at the Pillar
- The Crowning with the Thorns
- The Carrying of the Cross
- The Crucifixion and Death.

Introduction

We turn to the Lord, who knows our suffering and longs to give us his comfort and peace. Yet it was our infirmities that he bore, our sufferings that he endured. Isaiah 53:4a

Apostles' Creed

While we thought of him as stricken, as one smitten by God and afflicted. Isaiah 53:4b

Our Father...

Because God did not make death, nor does he rejoice in the destruction of the living. Wisdom 1:13

Hail Mary ...

For he fashioned all things that they might have being; and the creatures of the world are wholesome, Wisdom 1:14a

Hail Mary ...

And there is not a destructive drug among them nor any domain of the nether world on earth, Wisdom 1:14b

Hail Mary ...

For justice is undying. Wisdom 1:15

Glory Be...

The Agony in the Garden

Then going out [Jesus] went, as was his custom, to the Mount of Olives, and the disciples followed him. Luke 22:39

Our father...

When he arrived at the place he said to them, "Pray that you may not undergo the test." Luke 22:40

Hail Mary ...

After withdrawing about a stone's throw from them and kneeling, he prayed, saying, "Father, if you are willing, take this cup away from me; still, not my will but yours be done." Luke 22:41-42

Hail Mary ...

And to strengthen him an angel from heaven appeared to him. Luke 22:43

Hail Mary ...

He was in such agony and he prayed so fervently that his sweat became like drops of blood falling on the ground. Luke 22:44

Hail Mary ...

The spirit is willing, but the flesh is weak. Matthew 26:41b

Hail Mary ...

I cry aloud to God, cry to God to hear me. Psalm 77:2

Hail Mary ...

On the day of my distress I seek the Lord; by night my hands are raised unceasingly; I refuse to be consoled. Psalm 77:3

Hail Mary ...

My eyes cannot close in sleep; I am troubled and cannot speak. Psalm 77:5

Hail Mary ...

In the night I meditate in my heart; I ponder and my spirit broods: Psalm 77:7bc

Hail Mary ...

Has, God's love ceased forever? Has the promise failed for all ages? Psalm 77:9

Hail Mary ...

Has God forgotten mercy, in anger withheld compassion? Psalm 77:10

Glory Be...

The Scourging at the Pillar

Pilate addressed them a third time, "What evil has this man done? I found him guilty of no capital crime." Luke 23:22a

Our Father...

"Therefore I shall have him flogged and then release him." Luke 23:22b

Hail Mary ...

With loud shouts, however, they persisted in calling for his crucifixion, and their voices prevailed. Luke 23:23

Hail Mary ...

The verdict of Pilate was that their demand should be granted. Luke 23:24

Hail Mary ...

Then Pilate took Jesus and had him scourged. John 19:1

Hail Mary ...

So he released the man who had been imprisoned for rebellion and murder, for whom they asked, and he handed Jesus over to them to deal with as they wished. Luke 23:25

Hail Mary ...

How lonely she is now, the once crowded city! Lamentations 1:1a

Hail Mary ...

Widowed is she who was mistress over nations. Lamentations 1:1b

Hail Mary ...

The princess among the provinces has been made a toiling slave. Lamentations 1:1c

Hail Mary ...

Bitterly she weeps at night, tears upon her cheeks. Lamentations 1:2a

Hail Mary ...

With not one to console her of all her dear ones. Lamentations 1:2b

Hail Mary ...

Her friends have all betrayed her and become her enemies. Lamentations 1:2c

Glory Be...

The Crowning with Thorns

Then the soldiers of the governor took Jesus inside the praetorium and gathered the whole cohort around him. Matthew 27:27

Our father...

They stripped off his clothes and threw a scarlet military cloak about him. Matthew 27:28

Hail Mary ...

Weaving a crown out of thorns, they placed it on his head, and a reed in his right hand. Matthew 27:29a

Hail Mary ...

And kneeling before him, they mocked him, saying, "Hail, King of the Jews!" Matthew 27:29b

Hail Mary ...

They spat upon him and took the reed and kept striking him on the head. Matthew 27:30

Hail Mary ...

And when they had mocked him, they stripped him of the cloak, dressed him in his own clothes, and led him off to crucify him. Matthew 27:31

Hail Mary ...

Lord, my God, I call out by day; at night I cry aloud in your presence. Psalm 88:2

Hail Mary ...

You plunged me into the bottom of the pit, into the darkness of the abyss. Psalm 88:7

Hail Mary ...

All day I call on you, Lord; I stretch out my hands to you. Psalm 88:10bc

Hail Mary ...

Why do you reject me, Lord? Why hide your face from me? Psalm 88:15

Hail Mary ...

All the day they surge round like a flood; from every side they close in on me. Psalm 88:18

Hail Mary ...

Because of you companions shun me; my only friend is darkness. Psalm 88:19

Glory Be...

The Carrying of the Cross

As they led [Jesus] away they took hold of a certain Simon, a Cyrenian, who was coming in from the country; and after laying the cross on him, they made him carry it behind Jesus. Luke 23:26

Our Father...

A large crowd of people followed Jesus, including many women who mourned and lamented him. Luke 23:27

Hail Mary ...

Jesus turned to them and said, "Daughters of Jerusalem, do not weep for me; weep instead for yourselves and for your children. Luke 23:28

Hail Mary ...

"The days are coming when people will say, Blessed are the barren, the wombs that never bore and the breasts that never nursed.'" Luke 23: 29

Hail Mary ...

"At that time people will say to the mountains, Fall upon us!' and to the hills, Cover us!'" Luke 23:30

Hail Mary ...

"For if these things are done when the wood is green what will happen when it is dry?" Luke 23:31

Hail Mary ...

[Jesus said,] "Whoever wishes to come after me must deny himself, take up his cross, and follow me." Mark 8:34

Hail Mary ...

This, rather, is the fasting that I wish: releasing those bound unjustly, untying the thongs of the yoke; Setting free the oppressed, breaking every yoke. Isaiah 58:6

Hail Mary ...

Sharing your bread with the hungry, sheltering the oppressed and the homeless. Isaiah 58:7ab

Hail Mary ...

Clothing the naked when you see them, and not turning your back on your own. Isaiah 58:7cd

Hail Mary ...

Then your light shall break forth like the dawn, and your wound shall quickly be healed. Isaiah 58:8ab

Hail Mary ...

Then you shall call and the Lord will answer, you shall cry for help, and he will say: Here I am! Isaiah 58:9ab

Glory Be...

The Crucifixion

When they came to the place called the Skull, they crucified him and the criminals there, one on his right, the other on his left. Luke 23:33

Our Father...

Then Jesus said, "Father, forgive them, they know not what they do." Luke 23:34

Hail Mary ...

"Jesus, remember me when you come into your kingdom." Luke 23:42

Hail Mary ...

And about three o'clock Jesus cried out in a loud voice, "Eli, Eli, lema sabachthani?" which means, "My God, my God, why have you forsaken me?" Matthew 27:46

Hail Mary ...

Jesus cried out in a loud voice, "Father, into your hands I commend my spirit." Luke 23:46

Hail Mary ...

And bowing his head, he handed over the spirit. John 19:30b

Hail Mary ...

Do not hide your face from me; do not repel your servant in anger. You are my help; do not cast me off; do not forsake me, God my savior! Psalm 27:9

Hail Mary ...

But I believe I shall enjoy the Lord's goodness in the land of the living. Psalm 27:13

Hail Mary ...

Wait for the Lord, take courage; be stouthearted, wait for the Lord! Psalm 27:14

Hail Mary ...

But the souls of the just are in the hand of God, and no torment shall touch them. Wisdom 3:1

Hail Mary ...

They seemed, in the view of the foolish, to be dead; and their passing away was thought an affliction. Wisdom 3:2

Hail Mary ...
But they are in peace. Wisdom 3:3b

Glory Be...

Conclusion

"Amen, amen, I say to you, unless a grain of wheat falls to the ground and dies, it remains just a grain of wheat; but if it dies, it produces much fruit. Whoever loves his life loses it, and whoever hates his life in this world will preserve it for eternal life." John 12:24-25

THE GLORIOUS MYSTERIES

The glorious mysteries of the Rosary are prayed on Wednesday and Sunday. They are:

- The Resurrection of Jesus Christ
- The Ascension of Jesus to Heaven
- The Descent of the Holy Ghost
- The Assumption of the Blessed Virgin Mary into Heaven
- The Coronation of the Blessed Virgin Mary, Queen of Heaven and Earth.

The Resurrection of Jesus Christ

In the end of the Sabbath, as it began to dawn toward the first day of the week, came Mary Magdalene and the other Mary to see the sepulcher. And, behold, there was a great earthquake: for the angel of the Lord descended from heaven, and came and rolled back the stone from the door, and sat upon it. And the angel answered and said unto the women: *"Fear not ye! For I know that ye seek Jesus, which was crucified. He is not here. For he is risen, as he said". (Mat 28,1-6)*

The risen Jesus has proved that man, together with Him, can have power over sin and therefore death. Jesus, help raise us, deliver us from sin, from evil, give us Your light, give us Your joy. Rekindle inside us the love, the faith, the hopefulness, and the gift of prayer. Let us ask Mary for the gift of an unshakeable faith.

Our Lord Jesus Christ, on the third day after his passion and death, rose again in glory, victorious over death and never to die again.

Prayer Intentions:
- That all who are dying might join themselves with Christ who died and rose for them
- For those who do not believe

Our father...

O Holy Mary, hear the cries of those who are dying of AIDS...

Hail Mary, full of grace...

O Holy Mary, with a mother's care look gently on those who suffer with cancer...

Hail Mary, full of grace...

O Holy Mary, cradle the bodies broken with cares of this world...

Hail Mary, full of grace...

O Holy Mary, intercede for those imprisoned by selfishness and sin...

Hail Mary, full of grace...

O Holy Mary, remember those locked in their homes by fear...

Hail Mary, full of grace…

O Holy Mary, look with love on those whose minds betray them…

Hail Mary, full of grace…

O Holy Mary, hear the cry of those who wake to pain…

Hail Mary, full of grace…

O Holy Mary, stand by those who care for people who have grown old…

Hail Mary, full of grace…

O Holy Mary, comfort those must bury their loved one today…

Hail Mary, full of grace…

O Holy Mary, stand vigil by those who are about to die…

Hail Mary, full of grace…

Glory to the Father, and to the Son, and to the Holy Spirit:

as it was in the beginning, is now, and will be for ever. Amen.

The Ascension of Jesus to Heaven

And as they are speaking these things, Jesus Himself stood in the midst of them, and saith to them, "Peace to you"; being amazed, and becoming affrighted, they were thinking themselves to see a spirit. And he said to them, "Why are ye troubled? And wherefore do reasonings come up in your hearts? See my hands and my feet, that I am he; handle me and see, because a spirit hath not flesh and bones, as ye, see me having." And having said this, he shewed to them the hands and the feet. ... *"And, lo, I do send the promise of my Father upon you, but ye -- abide ye in the city of Jerusalem till ye be clothed with power from on high." And he led them forth without -- unto Bethany, and having lifted up His hands he did bless them, and it came to pass, in His blessing them, he was parted from them, and was borne up to the heaven. (Luk 24, 36-51)*

Jesus, You have not deserted Your apostles in anguish, but have given them the joy of knowing Jesus "glorified" over 40 days. After Your Ascension, You granted to all those who seek You the gift of recieving you in the Eucharist. Through Mary we trust in you. Mary, give us the gift of hope.

Our Lord Jesus Christ, forty days after his Resurrection, ascended into heaven with triumph and great glory, in the sight of his most holy mother and all his disciples.

Prayer Intentions:

- For run-aways, throw-aways and children who live on the street
- For all who have lost faith

Our Father...

O Holy Mary, hear the cries of those who mourn the dead...

Hail Mary, full of grace...

O Holy Mary, with a mother's care look gently on parents who bury their children...

Hail Mary, full of grace...

O Holy Mary, cradle the lives of those addicted or imprisoned...

Hail Mary, full of grace...

O Holy Mary, intercede for those who seek to live the Gospel of Life...

Hail Mary, full of grace...

O Holy Mary, remember those who have left home...

Hail Mary, full of grace...

O Holy Mary, look with love on young mothers who are afraid...

Hail Mary, full of grace...

O Holy Mary, hear the prayers of those who seek to make our country just...

Hail Mary, full of grace...

O Holy Mary, stand by those who fear their growing old...

Hail Mary, full of grace...

O Holy Mary, lead the children who are lost home to those who love them...

Hail Mary, full of grace...

O Holy Mary, embrace the orphan and the widow with your love...

Hail Mary, full of grace...

Glory to the Father, and to the Son, and to the Holy Spirit:

as it was in the beginning, is now, and will be for ever. Amen.

The Descent of the Holy Ghost (Pentecost)

And when the day of Pentecost was fully come, they were all with one accord in one place. And suddenly there came a sound from heaven as of a rushing mighty wind, and it filled all the house where they were sitting. And there appeared unto them cloven tongues like as of fire, and it sat upon each of them. And they were all filled with the Holy Ghost, and began to speak with other tongues, as the Spirit gave them utterance. (Act 2,1-4)

Jesus, inffuse us with the Comforter, the Holy Ghost, enlighten us with the light of Your Spirit, with His strength enter in the deepest parts of our hearts and heal us. Deliver us, fill up our hearts with Your love. Make us apostles of Yours, dear Lord. Let us ask Mary the gift of true love, the gift of prayer from the heart.

"Come Holy Spirit, come by means of the powerful intercession of the Immaculate Heart of Mary, Your well-beloved Spouse."

Our Lord Jesus Christ, sitting at the right hand of the Father, sent the Holy Spirit into the upper chamber where the apostles were gathered together, with the most Holy Virgin Mary.

Prayer Intentions:
- For those whose lives are given in the defense of life
- For all who study and preach the Gospel of Life

Our Father...

O Holy Mary, hear the cries of those who accept the call to fatherhood...

Hail Mary, full of grace...

O Holy Mary, with a mother's care guide all young women in love and in the truth...

Hail Mary, full of grace...

O Holy Mary, cradle the bodies of those who are dying in pain...

Hail Mary, full of grace...

O Holy Mary, intercede for those who seek to be good parents...

Hail Mary, full of grace...

O Holy Mary, remember the children of those who are dying...

Hail Mary, full of grace...

O Holy Mary, hear the cry of those whom we have forgotten...

Hail Mary, full of grace...

O Holy Mary, pray for all doctors that they may embrace a spirit of life...

Hail Mary, full of grace...

O Holy Mary, stand by those who are in despair...

Hail Mary, full of grace...

O Holy Mary, guide those tempted by sin and death...

Hail Mary, full of grace...

O Holy Mary, inspire all women by your example of faith...

Hail Mary, full of grace...

Glory to the Father, and to the Son, and to the Holy Spirit:

as it was in the beginning, is now, and will be for ever. Amen.

The Assumption of the Blessed Virgin Mary into Heaven

Blessed art thou of the most high God above all the women upon the earth; and blessed be the Lord God, which hath created the heavens and the earth, which hath directed thee to the cutting off of the head of the chief of our enemies. ... *Thou hast done all these things by thine hand: thou hast done much good to Israel, and God is pleased therewith: blessed be thou of the Almighty Lord for evermore. And all the people said, So be it. (Jdt 13,18-20; 15,10)*

Now that Mary is raised into heaven, She prays for Her sons and daughters, those sons and daughters Jesus left Her when He was on the cross. Mary, pray for us, You know our fears, take us into Your Heart, the Heart of a Mother. Help us now and in the time of our death to be with You in Heaven. We ask of you a devotion to Your Immaculate Heart, where we may take refuge in times of trouble.

The Most Holy Virgin, twelve years after the Resurrection of Our Lord Jesus Christ, passed from this life, and was assumed by the angels into heaven.

Prayer Intentions:

- That those who have gone before us in faith might rest in the Lord

- For babies who have died through abortion

Our father...

O Holy Mary, hear the cries of the mother whose child has been aborted...

Hail Mary, full of grace...

O Holy Mary, with a mother's care strengthen those who have grown weak with age...

Hail Mary, full of grace...

O Holy Mary, cradle the children who have died through our neglect...

Hail Mary, full of grace...

O Holy Mary, intercede for those abused or forgotten...

Hail Mary, full of grace...

O Holy Mary, remember those imprisoned by selfishness or sin...

Hail Mary, full of grace...

O Holy Mary, look with love on those who long for heaven...

Hail Mary, full of grace...

O Holy Mary, hear the prayers of doctors who seek to heal...

Hail Mary, full of grace...

O Holy Mary, stand by those who work to save the weakest and littlest among us...

Hail Mary, full of grace...

O Holy, Mary, intercede for all who love life and work to protect it...

Hail Mary, full of grace...

O Holy Mary, Teach us by your life to embrace Christ your son...

Hail Mary, full of grace...

Glory to the Father, and to the Son, and to the Holy Spirit:

as it was in the beginning, is now, and will be for ever. Amen.

The Coronation of the Blessed Virgin Mary, Queen of Heaven and Earth.

There appeared a great sign in heaven: a woman clothed with the sun, with the moon under her feet, and on her head a crown of twelve stars. (Rev 12,1)

Let us trust in Mary, Let us call to Her, let us love Her, let us confide in Her, because She gives Her all to us. We have a Mother in Heaven who is also a Queen; thus we need to turn to Her with full faith and hopefulness. If we ask for something while praying the Holy Rosary, it will be granted to us. Ask Her for the gift of prayer, a prayer of the heart, said only for love, a love for Her and Jesus. Let us also ask for a consistency of prayer, to always be joined to Her Heart, and therefore to the Heart of Jesus.

The Most Holy Virgin was crowned in heaven by her divine Son as the saints rejoiced in glory around her throne.

Prayer Intentions:

- *For all mothers, that they come to know the wonder of their vocation*
- *For all who are homeless, broken or afraid*

Our father...

O Holy Mary, hear the cries of those who long for heaven...

Hail Mary, full of grace...

O Holy Mary, with a mother's care lead the dying gently home...

Hail Mary, full of grace...

O Holy Mary, walk with those who seek the way home to your Son...

Hail Mary, full of grace...

O Holy Mary, intercede for those who pray to you today...

Hail Mary, full of grace...

O Holy Mary, remember those who lead and govern us...

Hail Mary, full of grace…

O Holy Mary, look with love on those who honor the name of your Son…

Hail Mary, full of grace…

O Holy Mary, send an angel to protect all who are lost…

Hail Mary, full of grace…

O Holy Mary, pray for the conversion of all who take life by violence…

Hail Mary, full of grace…

O Holy Mary, intercede with your son for all who have lost their way…

Hail Mary, full of grace…

O Holy Mary, walk closely with us in our search for the truth…

Hail Mary, full of grace…

Glory to the Father, and to the Son, and to the Holy Spirit:

as it was in the beginning, is now, and will be for ever. Amen.

CHAPTER 5
POWER AND PERSONAL TESTIMONIES OF THE ROSARY
PERSONAL TESTIMONIES OF THE ROSARY

So much of the power of the Rosary lies in its mysterious nature. This nature has been exemplified through many personal testimonies and stories over the years. Here will be given space to share various stories of the Rosary and how its power has influenced the people of God.

Here are a few personal testimonies that manifest the power of the *Rosary*.

The Power of the Rosary in converting Protestants

A little six-year-old Protestant boy had often heard his Catholic companion reciting the prayer 'Hail Mary.' He liked it so much that he copied it, memorized it and would recite it every day. 'Look, Mummy, what a beautiful prayer,' he said to his mother one day. 'Never again say it,' answered the mother.' It is a superstitious prayer of Catholics who adore idols and think Mary, a goddess. After all, she is a woman like any other. Come on, take this Bible and read it. It contains everything that we are bound to do and have to do.'

From that day on, the little boy discontinued his daily 'Hail Mary' and gave himself more time to reading the Bible instead. One day, while reading the Gospel, he came across the passage about the Annunciation of the Angel to Our Lady. Full of joy, the little boy ran to his mother and said: 'Mummy, I have found the 'Hail Mary' in the Bible which says: 'Hail Mary full of grace, the Lord is with thee, blessed art thou amongst women. ' Why do you call it a superstitious prayer?'

On another occasion, he found that beautiful Salutation of St. Elizabeth to The Virgin Mary and the wonderful canticle. MAGNIFICAT in which Mary foretold that 'the generations would call her blessed.' He said no more about it to his mother but started to recite the 'Hail Mary' every day as before. He felt pleasure in addressing those charming words to the Mother of Jesus, our Savior.

When he was fourteen, one day, he heard a discussion on Our Lady among the members of his family. Every one said that Mary was a common woman like any other woman. The boy, after listening to their erroneous reasoning, could not bear it any longer, and full of indignation, he interrupted them, saying: 'Mary is not like any other children of Adam, stained with sin. No! The Angel called her ***FULL OF GRACE AND BLESSED AMONGST WOMEN.*** Mary is the Mother of Jesus Christ and consequently

Mother of God. There is no higher dignity to which a creature can be raised.

The Gospel says that, the generations will proclaim her blessed and you are trying to despise her and look down on her. Your spirit is not the Spirit Of the Gospel or of the Bible which you proclaim to be the foundation of the Christian religion.' So deep was the impression which the boy's talk had made that his mother many times cried out sorrowfully: 'Oh my God! I fear that this son of mine will one day join the Catholic religion, the religion of Popes!' And indeed, not very long afterwards, having made a serious study of both Protestantism and Catholicism, the boy found the latter to be the only true religion and embraced it and became one of its most ardent apostles.

Some time after his conversion, he met his married sister who rebuked his and said indignantly: 'You little know how much I love my children. Should any one of them desire to become a Catholic, I would sooner pierce his heart with a dagger than allow him to embrace the religion of the Popes!' Her anger and temper were as furious as those of St. Paul before his conversion. However, she would change her ways, just as St. Paul did on his way to Damascus.

It so happened that one of her sons fell dangerously ill and the doctors gave up hope of recovery. Her brother then approached, her and spoke to her affectionately, saying: 'My dear sister, you naturally wish to have your child cured. Very well, then, do what I ask you to do. Follow me, let us pray one 'Hail Mary' and promise God that, if your son recovers his health, you would seriously study the Catholic doctrine, and should you come to the conclusion that Catholicism is the only true religion, you would embrace it no matter what the sacrifices may be.'

His sister was somewhat reluctant at the beginning but as she wished for her son's recovery. She accepted her brother's proposal and recited the 'Hail Mary' together with him. The next day her son was completely cured! The mother fulfilled her promise and she studied the Catholic doctrine. After long preparation she received Baptism together with her family, thanking her brother for being an apostle to her.

What I am I owe to Our Lady. You, too, my dear brethren, be entirely dedicated also to Our Lady and never let a day pass without saying the beautiful prayer, 'Hail Mary,' and your Rosary. Ask her to enlighten the minds of Protestants who are separated from the true Church of Christ founded on the Rock (Peter) and 'against whom the gates of hell shall never prevail.

Here are some further personal selections of Holy Rosary Testimonies, recorded by Saint Louis de Montfort and edited by a choir monk named Br Sean:

1. Two little girls, who were sisters, were saying the Rosary very devoutly in front of their house. A beautiful lady suddenly

appeared, walked towards the younger girl, who was only about six or seven, took her by the hand, and led her away. Her elder sister was very startled and looked for the little girl everywhere. At last, still not having found her, she went home weeping and told her parents that her sister had been kidnapped. For three whole days, the poor father and mother sought the child without success.

At the end of the third day they found her at the front door looking extremely happy and pleased. Naturally, they asked her where on earth she had been, and she told them that the lady to whom she had been saying the Rosary had taken her to a lovely place where she had given her delicious things to eat. She said that the lady had also given her a baby boy to hold, that he was very beautiful, and that she had kissed him again and again.

The father and mother, who had been converted to the Catholic faith only a short time before, sent at once for the Jesuit Father who had instructed them for their reception into the Church and who had also taught them devotion to the Rosary. They told him everything that had happened, and it was this priest himself who told me this story. It all took place in Paraguay.

2. Saint Dominic, seeing that the gravity of people's sins was hindering the conversion of the Albigensians, withdrew into a forest near Toulouse, where he prayed continuously for

three days and three nights. During this time, he did nothing but weep and do harsh penances in order to appease the anger of God. He used his discipline so much that his body was lacerated, and finally he fell into a coma.

At this point, our Lady appeared to him, accompanied by three angels, and she said, "Dear Dominic, do you know which weapon the Blessed Trinity wants to use to reform the world?"

"Oh, my Lady," answered Saint Dominic, "you know far better than I do, because next to your Son Jesus Christ you have always been the chief instrument of our salvation."

Then our Lady replied, "I want you to know that, in this kind of warfare, the principal weapon has always been the Angelic Psalter, which is the foundation-stone of the New Testament. Therefore, if you want to reach these hardened souls and win them over to God, preach my Psalter."

So he arose, comforted, and burning with zeal for the conversion of the people in that district, he made straight for the cathedral. At once unseen angels rang the bells to gather the people together, and Saint Dominic began to preach.

At the very beginning of his sermon, an appalling storm broke out, the earth shook, the sun was darkened, and there was so much thunder and lightning that all were very much afraid. Even greater was their fear when, looking at a picture of our Lady exposed in a prominent place, they saw her raise her arms to heaven three times to call down God's vengeance upon them if they failed to be converted, to amend their lives, and seek the protection of the holy Mother of God.

God wished, by means of these supernatural phenomena, to spread the new devotion of the holy Rosary and to make it more widely known.

At last, at the prayer of Saint Dominic, the storm came to an end, and he went on preaching. So fervently and compellingly did he explain the importance and value of the Rosary that almost all the people of Toulouse embraced it and renounced their false beliefs. In a very short time, a great improvement was seen in the town; people began leading Christian lives and gave up their former bad habits.

> 3. Inspired by the Holy Spirit, instructed by the Blessed Virgin as well as by his own experience, Saint Dominic preached the Rosary for the rest of his life. He preached it by his example as well as by his sermons.

One day, he had to preach at Notre Dame in Paris, and it happened to be the feast of St. John the Evangelist. He was in a little chapel behind the high altar prayerfully preparing his sermon by saying the Rosary, as he always did, when our Lady appeared to him and said: "Dominic, even though what you have planned to say may be very good, I am bringing you a much better sermon."

Saint Dominic took in his hands the book our Lady gave him, read the sermon carefully and, when he had understood it and meditated on it, he gave thanks to her. When the time came, he went up into the pulpit and, in spite of the feast day, made no mention of Saint John other than to say that he had been found worthy to be the guardian of the Queen of Heaven. The congregation was made up of theologians and other eminent people, who were used to hearing unusual and polished discourses; but Saint Dominic told them that it was not his desire to give them a learned discourse, wise in the eyes of the world, but that he would speak in the simplicity of the Holy Spirit and with his forcefulness.

So he began preaching the Rosary and explained the Hail Mary word by word as he would to a group of children, and used the very simple illustrations which were in the book given him by our Lady.

4. Carthagena, the great scholar, quoting Blessed Alan de la Roche in *De Dignitate Psalterii*, describes how this took place.

"Blessed Alan writes that one day Father Dominic said to him in a vision, 'My son, it is good to preach; but there is always a danger of looking for praise rather than the salvation of souls. Listen care-fully to what happened to me in Paris, so that you may be on your guard against this kind of mistake. I was to preach in the great church dedicated to the Blessed Virgin, and I was particularly anxious to give a fine sermon, not out of pride, but because of the high intellectual stature of the congregation.

"'An hour before the time I had to preach, I was dutifully saying my Rosary - as I always did before giving a sermon - when I fell into ecstasy. I saw my beloved friend, the Mother of God, coming towards me with a book in her hand. "Dominic," she said, "your sermon for today may be very good indeed, but no matter how good it is, I have brought you one that is very much better."

"'Of course I was overjoyed, and I took the book and read every word of it. Just as our Lady had said, I found exactly the right things to say in my sermon, so I thanked her with all my heart.

"'When it was time to begin, I saw that the University of Paris had turned out in full force, as well as a large number of noblemen. They had all seen and heard of the great things that the good Lord had been doing through me.

"'I went up into the pulpit. It was the feast of Saint John the Evangelist, but all I said about him was that he had been found worthy to be the guardian of the Queen of Heaven. Then I addressed the congregation: "'My Lords and illustrious doctors of the University, you are accustomed to hearing learned sermons suited to your refined tastes. Now I do not want to speak to you in the scholarly language of human wisdom but, on the contrary, to show you the Spirit of Cod and his greatness.'" Here ends the quotation from Blessed Alan, after which Carthagena goes on to say in his own words, "Then Saint Dominic explained the Angelic Salutation to them, using simple comparisons and examples from everyday life."

> 5. Blessed Alan, according to Carthagena, mentioned several other occasions when our Lord and our Lady appeared to Saint Dominic to urge him and inspire him to preach the Rosary more and more in order to wipe out sin and convert sinners and heretics.

In another passage, Carthagena says, "Blessed Alan said our Lady revealed to him that, after she had appeared to Saint Dominic, her blessed Son appeared to him and said, 'Dominic, I rejoice to see that you are not relying on your own wisdom and that, rather than seek the empty praise of men, you are working with great humility for the salvation of souls.

"'But many priests want to preach thunderously against the worst kinds of sin at the very outset, failing to realize that before a sick person is given bitter medicine, he needs to be prepared by being put into the right frame of mind to really benefit by it.

"'That is why, before doing anything else, priests should try to kindle a love of prayer in people's hearts and especially a love of my Angelic Psalter. If only they would all start saying it and would really persevere, God in his mercy could hardly refuse to give them his grace. So I want you to preach my Rosary.'"

6. In another place Blessed Alan says, "All priests say a Hail Mary with the faithful before preaching, to ask for God's grace. They do this because of a revelation that Saint Dominic had from our Lady. 'My son,' she said one day, 'do not be surprised that your sermons fail to bear the results you had hoped for. You are trying to cultivate a piece of ground which has not had any rain. Now when God planned to renew the face of the earth, he started by sending down rain from heaven - and this was the Angelic Salutation. In this way, God reformed the world. "'So when you give a sermon, urge people to say my Rosary, and in this way, your words will bear much fruit for souls.'

"Saint Dominic lost no time in obeying, and from then on he exerted great influence by his sermons." (This last quotation is from "The Book of Miracles of the Holy rosary," written in Italian, also found in Justin's works, Sermon 143.)

7. Later on, when these trials were over, thanks to the mercy of God, our Lady told Blessed Alan to revive the former Confraternity of the Holy Rosary. Blessed Alan was one of the Dominican Fathers at the monastery at Dinan, in Brittany. He was an eminent theologian

and a famous preacher. Our Lady chose him because, since the Confraternity had originally been started in that province, it was fitting that a Dominican from the same province should have the honour of re-establishing it.

Blessed Alan began this great work [the Confraternity of the Holy Rosary] in 1460, after a special warning from our Lord. This is how he received that urgent message, as he himself tells it: One day when he was offering Mass, our Lord, who wished to spur him on to preach the holy rosary, spoke to him in the Sacred Host. "How can you crucify me again so soon?" Jesus said. "What did you say, Lord?" asked Blessed Alan, horrified. "You crucified me once before by your sins," answered Jesus, "and I would willingly be crucified again rather than have my Father offended by the sins you used to commit. You are crucifying me again now because you have all the learning and understanding that you need to preach my Mother's Rosary, and you are not doing it. If you only did that, you could teach many souls the right path and lead them away from sin. But you are not doing it, and so you yourself are guilty of the sins that they commit." This terrible reproach made Blessed Alan solemnly resolve to preach the Rosary unceasingly.

8. Our Lady also said to him one day to inspire him to preach the Rosary more and more, "You were a great sinner in your youth, but I

obtained the grace of your conversion from my Son. Had such a thing been possible, I would have liked to have gone through all kinds of suffering to save you, because converted sinners are a glory to me. And I would have done that also to make you worthy of preaching my Rosary far and wide."

Saint Dominic appeared to Blessed Alan as well and told him of the great results of his ministry: he had preached the Rosary unceasingly, his sermons had borne great fruit and many people had been converted during his missions.

He said to Blessed Alan, "See what wonderful results I have had through preaching the Rosary. You and all who love our Lady ought to do the same so that, by means of this holy practice of the Rosary, you may draw all people to the real science of the virtues."

9. The chronicles of St. Francis tell of a young friar who had the praiseworthy habit of saying [the Rosary] of our Lady every day before dinner. One day, for some reason or other, he did not manage to say it. The refectory bell had already been rung when he asked the Superior to allow him to say it before coming to the table, and, having obtained permission, he withdrew to his cell to pray.

After he had been gone a long time, the Superior sent another friar to fetch him, and he found him in his room bathed in a heavenly light in the presence of our Lady and two angels. Beautiful roses kept issuing from his mouth at each Hail Mary, and the two angels were taking them one by one and placing them on our Lady's head, while she smilingly accepted them. Finally, two other friars who had been sent to find out what had happened to the first two saw the same scene, and our Lady did not leave until the whole Rosary had been said.

> 10. Blessed Thomas of St. John was well known for his sermons on the holy rosary, and the devil, jealous of his success, tortured him so much that he fell ill and was sick for such a long time that the doctors gave him up. One night, when he really thought he was dying, the devil appeared to him in the most terrible form imaginable. There was a picture of our Lady near his bed; he looked at it and cried with all his heart and soul and strength, "Help me, save me, my dearest Mother." No sooner had he said this than the picture seemed to come alive and our Lady put out her hand, took him by the arm and said, "Do not be afraid, Thomas my son, here I am and I am going to save you; get up now and go on preaching my Rosary as you used to do. I promise to shield you from your enemies."

When our Lady said this, the devil fled and Blessed Thomas got up, finding himself in perfect health. He then thanked our Lady with tears of joy. He resumed his Rosary apostolate, and his sermons were wonderfully successful.

> 11. Our Lady not only blesses those who preach her Rosary but she highly rewards all those who, by their example, get others to say it. Alphonsus, King of Leon and Galicia, very much wanted all his servants to honour the Blessed Virgin by saying the Rosary, so he used to hang a large rosary on his belt, though he never said it himself. Nevertheless, his wearing it encouraged his courtiers to say the Rosary devoutly.

One day the King fell seriously ill and when he was given up for dead, he found himself, in spirit, before the judgment-seat of our Lord. Many devils were there accusing him of all the sins he had committed, and our Lord was about to condemn him when our Lady came forward to speak in his favour. She called for a pair of scales and had his sins placed in one of the balances, while she put the large rosary which he had always worn on the other scale, together with all the rosaries that had been said through his example. It was found that the Rosaries weighed more than his sins.

Looking at him with great kindness, our Lady said, "As a reward for the little service you did for me in wearing my rosary, I have obtained a great grace for you from my Son. Your life will be spared for a few more years. See that you spend those years wisely, and do penance."

When the King regained consciousness he cried out, "Blessed be the Rosary of the most holy Virgin Mary, by which I have been de-livered from eternal damnation."

After he had recovered his health, he spent the rest of his life in spreading devotion to the Rosary, and said it faithfully every day.

> 12. While St. Dominic was preaching the Rosary in Carcassone, a heretic made fun of his miracles and the fifteen mysteries of the Rosary, and this prevented other heretics from being converted. As a punishment, God allowed fifteen thousand devils to enter the man's body.

His parents took him to Father Dominic to be delivered from the evil spirits. He started to pray and he begged everyone who was there to say the Rosary out loud with him, and at each Hail Mary our Lady drove a hundred devils out of the man, and they came out in the form of red-hot coals.

After he had been delivered, he abjured his former errors, was converted and joined the Rosary Confraternity. Several of his associates did the same, having been greatly moved by his punishment and by the power of the Rosary.

> 13. The learned Franciscan, Carthagena, as well as several other authors, says that an extraordinary event took place in 1482. The venerable Fr. James Sprenger and the

religious of his order were zealously working to re-establish devotion to the Rosary and its Confraternity in the city of Cologne. Unfortunately, two priests who were famous for their preaching ability were jealous of the great influence they were exerting through preaching the Rosary. These two Fathers spoke against this devotion whenever they had a chance, and as they were very eloquent and had a great reputation, they persuaded many people not to join the Confraternity. One of them, the better to achieve his wicked end, wrote a special sermon against the Rosary and planned to give it the following Sunday. But when the time came for the sermon he did not appear and, after a certain amount of waiting, someone went to fetch him. He was found to be dead, and he had evidently died without anyone to help him.

After persuading himself that this death was due to natural causes, the other priest decided to carry out his friend's plan and give a similar sermon on another day, hoping to put an end to the Confraternity of the Rosary. However, when the day came for him to preach and it was time to give the sermon, God punished him by striking him down with paralysis which deprived him of the use of his limbs and of his power of speech.

At last he admitted his fault and that of his friend and in his heart he silently besought our Lady to help him.

He promised that if only she would cure him, he would preach the Rosary with as much zeal as that with which he had formerly fought against it. For this end he implored her to restore his health and his speech, which she did, and finding himself instantaneously cured he rose up like another Saul, a persecutor turned defender of the holy Rosary. He publicly acknowledged his former error, and ever afterwards preached the wonders of the Rosary with great zeal and eloquence.

> 14. One day, when St. Mechtilde was praying and was trying to think of some way in which she could express her love of the Blessed Virgin better than before, she fell into ecstasy. Our Lady appeared to her with the Angelic Salutation written in letters of gold upon her breast and said to her, "My daughter, I want you to know that no one can please me more than by saying the greeting which the most adorable Trinity presented to me and by which I was raised to the dignity of the Mother of God.

"By the word Ave, which is the name of Eve, Eva, I learned that God in his infinite power had preserved me from all sin and its attendant misery which the first woman had been subject to.

"The name Mary, which means 'lady of light,' shows that God has filled me with wisdom and light, like a shining star, to light up heaven and earth.

"The words, full of grace, remind me that the Holy Spirit has showered so many graces upon me that I am able to give these graces in abundance to those who ask for them through my mediation.

"When people say, The Lord is with thee, they renew the indescribable joy that was mine when the eternal Word became incarnate in my womb.

"When you say to me, Blessed art thou among women, I praise the mercy of God who has raised me to this exalted degree of happiness.

"And at the words, Blessed is the fruit of thy womb, Jesus, the whole of heaven rejoices with me to see my Son Jesus adored and glorified for having saved mankind." Seventeenth Rose

> 15. Blessed Alan de la Roche, who was so deeply devoted to the Blessed Virgin, had many revelations from her, and we know that he confirmed the truth of these revelations by a solemn oath. Three of them stand out with special emphasis: the first, that if people fail to say the Hail Mary, which has saved the world, out of carelessness, or because they are lukewarm, or because they hate it, this is an indication that they will probably be condemned to eternal punishment.

The second truth is that those who love this divine salutation bear the very special stamp of predestination. The third is that those to whom God has given this favour of loving our Lady and of serving her out of love must take very great care to continue to love and serve her until the time when she shall have had them placed in heaven by her Son in the degree of glory which they have earned.

16. Blessed Alan also relates that a nun who had always had a great devotion to the Rosary appeared after her death to one of her sisters in religion and said to her, "If I were able to return in my body to have the chance of saying just a single Hail Mary, even without great fervor, I would gladly go through the sufferings that I had during my last illness all over again, in order to gain the merit of this prayer" It is to be noted that she had been bedridden and suffered agonizing pains for several years before she died.

17. Whatever you do, do not be like a certain pious but self-willed lady in Rome, so often referred to by speakers on the Rosary. She was so devout and fervent that she put to shame by her holy life even the strictest religious in the Church.

Having decided to ask St. Dominic's advice about her spiritual life, she made her confession to him. For penance he gave her one Rosary to say and advised her to say it every day. She excused herself, saying that she had her regular exercises, that she made the Stations of Rome every day, that she wore sack-cloth as well as a hair-shirt, that she gave herself the discipline several times a week, that she often fasted and did other penances. Saint Dominic urged her over and over again to take his advice and say the Rosary, but she would not hear of it. She left the confessional, horrified at the methods of this new spiritual director who had tried so hard to persuade her to take up a devotion for which she had no taste.

Later on, when she was at prayer she fell into ecstasy and had a vision of her soul appearing before the Supreme Judge. Saint Michael put all her penances and other prayers on one side of the scales and all her sins and imperfections on the other. The tray of her good works were greatly outweighed by that of her sins and imperfections.

Filled with alarm, she cried for mercy, imploring the help of the Blessed Virgin, her gracious advocate, who took the one and only Rosary she had said for her penance and dropped it on the tray of her good works. This one Rosary was so heavy that it weighed more than all her sins as well as all her good works. Our Lady then reproved her for having refused to follow the counsel of her servant Dominic and for not saying the Rosary every day.

As soon as she came to herself she rushed and threw herself at the feet of Saint Dominic and told him all that had happened, begged his forgiveness for her unbelief, and promised to say the Rosary faithfully every day. By this means she rose to Christian perfection and finally to the glory of everlasting life.

18. Few saints have reached the same heights of prayer as Saint Mary Magdalene, who was lifted up to heaven by angels each day, and who had the privilege of learning at the feet of Jesus and his holy Mother. Yet one day, when she asked God to show her a sure way of advancing in his love and arriving at the heights of perfection, he sent the archangel St. Michael to tell her, on his behalf, that there was no other way for her to reach perfection than to meditate on our Lord's passion. So he placed a cross in the front of her cave and told her to pray before it, contemplating the sorrowful mysteries which she had seen take place with her own eyes.

19. Blessed Alan relates that a man he knew had tried desperately all kinds of devotions to rid himself of the evil spirit which possessed him, but without success. Finally, he thought of wearing his rosary round his neck, which eased him considerably. He discovered that whenever he took it off the devil tormented him cruelly, so he resolved to wear it night and day. This drove the evil spirit away forever because he could not bear such a terrible chain. Blessed Alan also testifies that he delivered a great number of those who were possessed by putting a rosary round their necks.

20. Father Jean Amat, of the Order of St. Dominic, was giving a series of Lenten sermons in the Kingdom of Aragon one year, when a young girl was brought to him who was possessed by the devil. After he had exorcised her several times without success, he put his rosary round her neck. Hardly had he done so when the girl began to scream and cry out in a fearful way, shrieking, "Take it off, take it off; these beads are tormenting me." At last, the priest, filled with pity for the girl, took his rosary off her.

The very next night, when Fr. Amat was in bed, the same devils who had possession of the girl came to him, foaming with rage and tried to seize him. But he had his rosary clasped in his hand and no efforts of theirs could wrench it from him. He beat them with it very well indeed and put them to flight, crying out, "Holy Mary, Our Lady of the Rosary, come to my help."

The next day on his way to the church, he met the poor girl, still possessed; one of the devils within her started to jeer at him, saying, "Well, brother, if you had been without your rosary, we should have made short shrift of you." Then, the good Father, threw his rosary round the girl's neck without more ado, saying, "By the sacred names of Jesus and Mary his holy Mother, and by the power of the holy Rosary, I command you, evil spirits, to leave the body of this girl at once." They were immediately forced to obey him, and she was delivered from them.

21. Our Lady one day revealed to Blessed Alan de la Roche that, after the holy sacrifice of the Mass, which is the first and most living memorial of our Lord's passion, there was indeed no more excellent devotion or one of greater merit than that of the Rosary, which is like a second memorial and representation of the life and passion of Jesus Christ.

22. Fr. Dorland relates that in 1481 our Lady appeared to the Venerable Dominic, a Carthusian devoted to the holy Rosary, who lived at Treves, and said to him: "Whenever one of the faithful, in a state of grace, says the Rosary while meditating on the mysteries of the life and passion of Christ, he obtains full and entire remission of all his sins."

She also said to Blessed Alan, "I want you to know that, although there are numerous indulgences already attached to the recitation of my Rosary, I shall add many more to every five decades for those who, free from serious sin, say them with devotion, on their knees. And whosoever shall persevere in the devotion of the holy rosary, with it, s prayers and meditations, shall be rewarded for it; I shall obtain for him full remission of the penalty and the guilt of all his sins at the end of his life.

"And let this not seem incredible to you; it is easy for me because I am the Mother of the King of heaven, and he calls me full of grace. And being filled with grace, I am able to dispense it freely to my dear children."

23. The saintly Blanche of Castille, Queen of France, was deeply grieved because twelve years after her marriage she was still childless. When St. Dominic went to see her he advised her to say the Rosary every day to ask God for the grace of motherhood, and she faithfully carried out his advice. In the year 1213, she gave birth to her eldest child, who was called Philip. But when the child died in infancy, the Queen sought our Lady's help more than ever, and had a large number of rosaries given out to all members of the court and to people in several towns in the Kingdom, asking them to pray to God for a blessing which this time would be complete. This was granted to her, for in 1215, St. Louis was born, the prince who was to become the glory of France and the model of Christian kings.

24. Alphonsus VIII, King of Aragon and Castille, had been leading a disorderly life and had been punished by God in several ways, and he was forced to take refuge in a town belonging to one of his allies.

St. Dominic happened to be in this town on Christmas Day and he preached on the Rosary as he usually did, and spoke of the graces that we obtain through this devotion. He mentioned, among other things, that those who said the Rosary devoutly would overcome their enemies and regain all they had lost.

The King listened attentively and sent for St. Dominic to ask whether what he had said about the Rosary was really true. The Saint assured him that nothing was more true, and that if only he would practice this devotion and join the Confraternity, he would see for himself. The King resolved to say the Rosary every day and persevered for a year in doing so. The very next Christmas, our Lady appeared to him at the end of his Rosary and said, "Alphonsus, you have served me for a year by saying my Rosary devoutly every day, so I have come to reward you. I have obtained the forgiveness of your sins from my Son. Here is a rosary, which I present to you; wear it, and I promise you that none of your enemies will be able to harm you."

Our Lady vanished, leaving the King overjoyed and greatly encouraged; he immediately went in search of the Queen and told her all about our Lady's gift and the promise that went with it. He touched her eyes with this rosary, for she had lost her sight, and she was cured.

Shortly afterwards, the King rallied some troops and with the help of his allies boldly attacked his enemies. He forced them to give back the territory they had taken from him and make reparation for his losses. They were completely routed, and he became so successful in war that soldiers came from all sides to fight under his standard because it seemed that, whenever he went into battle, the victory was sure to be his.

This is not surprising because he never went into battle without first saying his Rosary on his knees. He made certain that the whole of his court joined the Confraternity of the Rosary and he saw to it that all his officials and servants were devoted to it.

The Queen also joined the Confraternity, and they both persevered in the service of Blessed Virgin and lived very holy lives.

> 25. St. Dominic had a cousin named Don Perez or Pedro, who was leading a highly immoral life. When he heard that his cousin was preaching on the wonders of the Rosary and learned that several people had been converted and had amended their lives by means of it, he said, "I had given up all hope of being saved, but now I am beginning to take heart again. I really must hear this man of God."

So one day he went to hear one of St. Dominic's sermons. When the latter caught sight of him, he struck out against sin more zealously than ever before, and from the depths of his heart he besought

God to enlighten his cousin and let him see what a deplorable state his soul was in.

At first, Don Perez was somewhat alarmed, but he still did not resolve to change his ways. He came once more to hear the Saint preach and his cousin, realizing that a heart as hardened as his could only be moved by something extraordinary, cried out with a loud voice, "Lord Jesus, grant that this whole congregation may see the state of the man who has just come into your house."

Then everyone suddenly saw that Don Perez was completely surrounded by a band of devils in the form of hideous beasts, who were holding him in great iron chains. People fled in all directions in abject terror, and Don Perez himself was even more appalled when he saw how everyone shunned him. St. Dominic told them all to stand still and said to his cousin, "Unhappy man that you are, acknowledge the deplorable state you are in and throw yourself at our Lady's feet. Take this rosary, say it with devotion and with true sorrow for all your sins, and make a resolution to amend your life."

Don Perez knelt down and said the Rosary; he then felt the desire to make his confession, which he did with heartfelt contrition. St. Dominic ordered him to say the Rosary every day; he promised to do this and he entered his own name in the register of the Confraternity. When he left the church his face was no longer horrible to behold but shining like that of an angel. Thereafter he persevered in devotion to the

Rosary, led a well-ordered life and died a happy death.

    26. When St. Dominic was preaching the Rosary near Carcassone, an Albigensian was brought to him who was possessed by the devil. The Saint exorcised him in the presence of a great crowd of people; it appears that over twelve thousand had come to hear him speak. The devils who were in possession of this wretched man were forced to answer St. Dominic's questions in spite of themselves.

They said:

- That there were fifteen thousand of them in the body of that poor man, because he had attacked the fifteen mysteries of the Rosary;
- That by the Rosary which he preached, he put fear and horror into the depths of hell, and that he was the man they hated most throughout the world because of the souls he snatched from them by the devotion of the Rosary.
- They revealed several other things.

    27. St. Dominic put his rosary round the neck of the possessed man and asked them who, of all the saints in heaven, was the one they feared most, who should, therefore, be the most loved and revered by men.

At this, they let out such unearthly screams that most of the people fell to the ground, seized with fear. Then, using all their cunning so as not to answer, the devils wept and wailed in such a pitiful way that many of the people wept also, out of pure natural pity. The devils, speaking through the mouth of the Albigensian, pleaded in a heart-rending voice, "Dominic, Dominic, have pity on us, we promise you we will never harm you. "You have always had compassion for sinners and those in distress; have pity on us, for we are in grievous straits. We are suffering so much already, why do you delight in increasing our pains? Can't you be satisfied with the pains we now endure? Have mercy on us, have mercy on us!"

28. St. Dominic was not in the least moved by the pathetic words of those wretched spirits and told them he would not let them alone until they had answered his question. Then they said they would whisper the answer in such a way that only St. Dominic would be able to hear. The latter firmly insisted upon their answering clearly and audibly. Then, the devils, kept quiet and would not, say another word, completely disregarding St. Dominic's orders.

So he knelt down and said this prayer to our Lady: "Oh, most glorious Virgin Mary, I implore you by the power of the holy rosary command these enemies of the human race to answer my question."

No sooner had he said this prayer than a glowing flame leaped out of the ears, nostrils and mouth of the possessed man. Everyone shook with fear, but the fire did not hurt anyone. Then the devils cried, "Dominic, we beseech you, by the passion of Jesus Christ and the merits of his holy Mother and of all the saints, let us leave the body of this man without speaking further; for the angels will answer your question whenever you wish. After all, are we not liars - so why should you want to believe us? Do not torment us any more, have pity on us."

"Woe to you, wretched spirits, who do not deserve to be heard," St. Dominic said, and kneeling down he prayed to the Blessed Virgin: "O most worthy Mother of Wisdom, I am praying for the people assembled here, who have already learned how to say the Angelic Salutation properly. I beg you for the salvation of those here present, compel these adversaries of yours to proclaim the whole truth here and now before the people."

St. Dominic had scarcely finished this prayer when he saw the Blessed Virgin near at hand surrounded by a multitude of angels. She struck the possessed man with a golden rod that she held and said, "Answer my servant Dominic at once." {It must be noted that the people neither saw nor heard our Lady, only St. Dominic}.

    29. Then the devils started screaming: "Oh, you who are enemy, our downfall and our destruction, why have you come from heaven

to torture us so grievously? O advocate of sinners, you who snatch them from the very jaws of hell, you who are a most sure path to heaven, must we, in spite of ourselves, tell the whole truth and confess before everyone who it is who is the cause of our shame and our ruin? Oh, woe to us, princes of darkness.

"Then listen, you Christians. This Mother of Jesus is most powerful in saving her servants from falling into hell. She is like the sun which destroys the darkness of our wiles and subtlety. It is she who uncovers our hidden plots, breaks our snares, and makes our temptations useless and ineffective.

"We have to say, however, reluctantly, that no soul who has really persevered in her service has ever been damned with us; one single sigh that she offers to the Blessed Trinity is worth far more than all the prayers, desires, and aspirations of all the saints. We fear her more than all the other saints in heaven together, and we have no success with her faithful servants.

"Many Christians who call on her at the hour of death and who really ought to be damned according to our ordinary standards are saved by her intercession. And if that Marietta (it is thus in their fury they called her) did not counter our plans and our efforts, we should have overcome the Church and destroyed it long before this, and caused all the Orders in the Church to fall into error and infidelity.

"Now that we are forced to speak, we must also tell you that nobody who perseveres in saying the Rosary will be damned because she obtains for her servants the grace of true contrition for their sins by which they obtain pardon and mercy."

Then, St. Dominic had all the people say the Rosary very slowly and with great devotion, and a wonderful thing happened: at each Hail Mary which he and the people said, a large number of devils issued forth from the wretched man's body under the guise of red-hot coals. When the devils had all been expelled and the heretic completely delivered from them, our Lady, although invisible, gave her blessing to the assembled company, and they were filled with joy.

A large number of heretics were converted because of this miracle and joined the Confraternity of the Holy Rosary.

> 30. It is almost impossible to do credit sufficiently to the victories that Count Simon de Montfort won against the Albigensians under the patronage of Our Lady of the Rosary. They are so famous that the world has never seen anything to match them. One day he defeated ten thousand heretics with a force of five hundred men; on another occasion he overcame three thousand with only thirty men; finally, with eight hundred horsemen and one thousand infantrymen he completely routed the army of the King of Aragon, which was a hundred thousand strong, and this with the loss on his side of only one horseman and eight soldiers

CONCLUSION

The fact that our Church continues to include the Feast of the Holy Rosary on the liturgical calendar testifies to the importance and goodness of this form of prayer. Archbishop Fulton Sheen said, *"The Rosary is the book of the blind, where souls see and there enact the greatest drama of love the world has ever known; it is the book of the simple, which initiates them into mysteries and knowledge more satisfying than the education of other men; it is the book of the aged, whose eyes close upon the shadow of this world, and open on the substance of the next. The power of the Rosary is beyond description."*

The Rosary is not only a Catholic devotion. Some Anglicans also pray the Rosary as well as one other Christians who want to develop a special relationship with Mary, as mother and fellow disciple. Their interpretation of the devotion may differ, but the Rosary is used. Some Lutherans also use the Rosary.

The Rosary can also be used for other special prayers and devotions. It's not just the Hail Mary. For example, a chaplet, or single decade devotions can be prayed and the beads used to count those prayers as well. This is an acceptable use of the Rosary.

There are few things worthy of embellishment in the world, all else being vanity. Churches are one of them, as well as our other religious relics, Rosaries included. This is because their embellishment -their enhancement as works of art, are reminders of the glory of God. Not all Christians understand this, but it is a distinctly Catholic understanding with ancient roots in the tradition of the Faith. In other words, it's perfectly okay to own a beautiful Rosary, just as it is okay for a community to adorn its Church with the most beautiful gifts and talents it possesses. God accepts us at our worst, so He is worthy of our best.

Printed in Great Britain
by Amazon